THE *Secret* OF THE SHADOW

ALSO BY DEBBIE FORD

The Dark Side of the Light Chasers
Spiritual Divorce

THE *Secret* OF THE SHADOW

The Power of Owning
Your Whole Story

DEBBIE FORD

HarperSanFrancisco
A Division of HarperCollins*Publishers*

HarperCollins books may be purchased for educational, business, or sales promotional use. For information please write: Special Markets Department, HarperCollins Publishers, Inc., 10 East 53rd Street, New York, NY 10022.

HarperCollins Web site: http://www.harpercollins.com
HarperCollins®, ♨®, and HarperSanFrancisco™ are trademarks of HarperCollins Publishers, Inc.

FIRST EDITION
Designed by Joseph Rutt

Library of Congress Cataloging-in-Publication Data
Ford, Debbie.
The secret of the shadow : the power of owning your whole story /
Debbie Ford. — 1st ed.
p. cm.
ISBN 0–06–251782–1 (paper)
1. Self-actualization (Psychology). I. Title.
BF637.S4 F65 2002
158.1—dc21   2001039784

02 03 04 05 06 ❖/RRD 10 9 8 7 6 5 4 3 2

To my dear second father, Howard J. Fuerst, M.D.
What a tremendous gift I received when you came into my life.
Thank you for all the care, love, and grace that you
brought to my family, the world, and me.
Know that you are deeply missed.

Contents

CONTENTS

Chapter 6
THE POWER OF PROCESS
101

Chapter 7
MAKING PEACE WITH YOUR STORY
127

Chapter 8
FINDING YOUR UNIQUE SPECIALTY
153

Chapter 9
LIVING OUTSIDE YOUR STORY
179

Chapter 10
THE SECRET OF THE SHADOW
197

ACKNOWLEDGMENTS
219

THE *Secret* OF THE
SHADOW

Chapter 1

YOU AND YOUR STORY

I magine that you knew at birth that you were a master, that you were powerful beyond measure, that you possessed enormous gifts, and that all it would take to deliver your gifts to the world was your desire. Imagine that you came into this world with your heart filled with the healing power of love and that your only desire was to bestow that love onto all those around you. Imagine that you had the innate ability to create and have all that you want and all that you need. Is it possible that at some point in your life you knew that there was no one else in the world like you? And that in every fiber of your being you knew that you not only possessed the light of the world, but that you were the light of the world? Is it possible that at one time you knew who you were at the deepest level and you rejoiced in your gifts? Take a moment now, and see if you can remember that time when you knew the truth of who you really are.

Then something happened. Your world changed. Something or someone cast a shadow on your light. From that moment on you feared that you and your precious gifts were no longer safe in the world. You felt that if you didn't hide your sacred gift it might be abused, injured, or taken away from you. Deep inside, you knew that this gift was like a precious, innocent child that was yours to protect. So you did what any good parent would do: You hid all your magnificence deep inside so that no one would ever discover it, so that no one could hurt it or take it away from you. Then, with the creativity of a child, you covered it up. You created an act, a persona, a drama, a story so that nobody would ever suspect that you were the keeper of so much light. You were very smart—brilliant, actually—at hiding your secret. Not only did you convince others that you were not that; you also convinced yourself—all because you were being a good parent to the gift that you held. It was your secret—your deep, dark secret, which only you knew. You were even creative enough to manifest the exact opposite of that which you truly are so that you could protect yourself from those who might be upset or angered by your innate gifts.

But after days, months, and years of hiding your precious treasure, you began to believe your story. You became the persona you created to protect your secret. At that moment you forgot that you had ever buried your treasured gift in the first place. You not only forgot where you had hidden it, you forgot that you had hidden it at all. Your light, love, greatness, and beauty got lost inside your story. You forgot that you had a secret.

From that moment on, you felt lost, alone, separate, and scared. Suddenly you became aware that there was something missing—and there was. The pain of separating from your treasure felt like losing your best friend. Inside, you ached for the return of your true self. So you began a search outside of yourself for something that would fill the void and make you feel better. You looked to relationships, to other people, to your achievements and awards, trying to find that which was missing. You looked to your body and your bank account, trying to get that feeling back. Maybe, like me, you were driven by feelings of unworthiness that ran so deep that you spent most of your life frantically searching for something to complete you. But everywhere you looked you came up empty.

By the time I was five years old, I was all too familiar with the voice in my head telling me that I wasn't good enough, that I wasn't wanted, and that I didn't belong. Desperate to feel loved and accepted, I set out on the exhausting task of getting other people to validate my worth. Deep inside I believed there was something wrong with me, and I went to great lengths to conceal my flaws. I quickly learned how to charm people, flashing my biggest smile to get them to notice me. I thought that if I was more talented than my older sister or smarter than my older brother, I would belong and my family would fill me with all the love and acceptance I hungered for. I believed that if they loved me enough, I would no longer have to listen to the awful thoughts that filled my mind or endure the painful feelings that consumed my small body.

As the years passed, I became skilled at finding ways to hide my pain from myself and others. When I couldn't find someone to validate me or tell me I was okay, I would sneak across the street to the nearby 7-Eleven and buy a package of Sara Lee brownies and a bottle of Coca-Cola. That dose of sugar really seemed to do the trick. But by the age of twelve my pain was too big to hide: I felt too tall, too awkward, and too stupid. I was envious of the girls who seemed to fit in, who wore the right clothes and had the right families. For years I cried every day, trying to release the inner pain that consumed me. My tears of sadness always had the same message: "Why doesn't anyone love me? What's wrong with me? Please, won't someone come and *help* me?"

Then, to make matters even worse, one Saturday afternoon when I was twelve years old my mother informed my brother and me that while we were at the beach, my father had moved out of the house. Their marriage was over, and they were going to get a divorce. The breakup of my family added to my deep-seated fear that I was flawed, damaged, and that I had been dealt a bad lot in life. My parents' divorce unleashed all the pain that was stored up inside me. In an instant every bad feeling I thought I had under control came flooding out of me. My pain was so overwhelming that to numb it I turned to drugs, cigarettes, and fast friends in a desperate attempt to fit in and get the love and safety I could not find in my family or myself.

Struggling to make meaning from the emptiness I felt inside, I decided that success was my ultimate ticket to freedom. I began working at age thirteen, and by the time I was nineteen I owned my first retail store. I had an eye for fashion, and I loved designing new looks for women to wear. Wearing cool clothes always made me feel better about myself. It seemed that I could cover up my shame, if only for a day, by wearing something everyone liked. I strove to have the coolest, hippest, most trendy looks so that I would finally feel like I belonged. And from all outer appearances I succeeded: I had the right car, the right clothes, and what I considered to be the right set of friends. I had finally made it as a member of the "in" crowd. But despite all my successes and all my friends, I still felt lost and incredibly lonely. No matter how much I accomplished in the outer world, I could never seem to get away from the internal voice that told me I would never amount to anything and that my life really didn't matter. In the quiet of the night, my despair overwhelmed me. I felt flawed, small, insignificant, and painfully alone.

Managing the insanity of my mind became a full-time job. I began trying to quiet the constant internal noise by drowning myself in drugs. I was hypnotized by my continuous internal dialogue, by the story I told myself over and over again about how I would never make it, how I would never have the love, security, and inner peace I so desperately desired. That voice filled my head day and night, criticizing my every move and sabotaging my search for success and happiness. I had thought that if I kept busy enough, ate enough brownies, added enough chemicals, or accumulated enough cars and clothes, I could rise above the despair and hopelessness that always seemed to pop up after a moment of joy. But it didn't work. The tape that played in my head would only get louder, showing me my faults and reinforcing my self-imposed limitations. That voice continually reprimanded me, telling me I didn't deserve love and that I would always be alone. Finally, exhausted, I would surrender to my inner tyrant, saying, "Okay, you win." I would then reach for a bag of M&M's, a cigarette, or a tranquilizer and temporarily pacify my angst. But it took only moments before the self-loathing would return and the story about how awful I was would pick up where it had left off.

In my early twenties I added men to my prescription for pain relief. Unfortunately, my relationships with men always seemed to backfire. They began with a high that held the promise of salvation and ended with a low that left me deeper in the hole than when I began. Meanwhile, my substance abuse escalated to a point where I knew I would not live much longer if I continued down that path. I spent years going in and out of drug-treatment centers, trying to straighten out my life. Then one day as I was sitting in my fourth treatment center, participating in yet another group-therapy session, a huge realization hit me. As I sat there listening to everyone share their pain, I became spellbound by their words. As other members of my group shared their trials and tribulations, their failures and disappointments, I heard a common theme—a story line—coming out of each person's mouth. I was amazed by how committed each person was to their individual painful drama, and how sure they were that their story was the truth, the whole truth, and nothing but the truth. I saw people in my group sacrifice love in order to pay homage and remain true to the negative story they told about their lives. I watched other people holding on, as if for dear life, to their miserable sagas, trying to convince us all of how bad and how true their stories were. Some people were proud of their stories, as if their struggles and sacrifices made them somehow superior to the rest of us. Others were drenched in self-righteousness by sheer virtue of the depth of their pain. Suddenly, in a flash of clarity, I was able to hear something underneath each person's saga: *Their stories were just that—stories, fictional tales whose repeated telling was a distraction masking a much deeper truth.*

I vividly remember one group session in particular. Jessica was a pretty, blond twenty-eight-year-old woman whose face hung low with bitterness and defeat. She began our session that day by dramatically reciting the same story she had been telling us for the past eight or nine weeks. It went something like this: "My mother doesn't love me, my father left me when I was three, my boyfriend doesn't know who I am . . ." I sat there frustrated, wanting to pull my hair out. I just couldn't listen to that same story for one more minute. She sounded like a broken record, playing over and over and over the same bad song. I thought the least she could do was play us a new tune. I wanted to stand up and scream, "Get out of your story! Don't you get it? Can't you see you are telling yourself a story that will always end the same way?!" I wanted so badly for Jessica to see that she was keeping herself stuck inside her dead-end tale. But of course I was bound by the limitations of what I now know was my *own* story, which told me, "You don't know anything. You don't know what you're talking about, so stay in your seat and keep your big mouth shut." Obeying that voice, I slouched back into my chair and slipped back deeper into my own story. My silence was itself proof that my story had complete power over me.

Since I couldn't bear to listen to Jessica whine for one more moment, I tuned her out and turned all my attention onto myself. As Jessica's voice faded into the background, I began to hear my own internal dialog: "Nobody loves me. I can't do this. I'll never be happy. I'm too skinny and too ugly. My life doesn't matter" and the ever familiar, "No one cares about me." As I was sitting there it struck me that, like Jessica, I too was repeating the same internal dialogue over and over, reciting a version of my life I had heard a million times before. I was shocked to discover that my story line wasn't that much different from Jessica's; she was just speaking hers aloud. As I sat there listening to myself, I heard the theme of my story, chanted like a mantra in my mind: "Poor me, poor me, poor me." Then suddenly the lights went on and I realized, "Oh, my God, my life is just a story, too."

Until that day, sitting in a treatment center in West Palm Beach, Florida, I had been asleep inside my story. I was letting my story run my life without my knowing it. Everything I did was consistent with and constricted by this story, and my actions were desperate attempts to make the prison of my story a little better, a little more palatable, a little more livable. I was always making some minor adjustment—a new boyfriend, a new job, a new haircut—in an attempt to bury my pain and hide the "evidence" of my inadequacy. I had so mistaken my story for reality that making all these changes was like rearranging the chairs on the deck of the *Titanic:* The ship was sinking while I, blinded to the reality of the situation, was busy trying to make it look good and feel better while it was going down.

It finally occurred to me that there must be more to me than the story I was telling myself. Just as I could see that Jessica, even while stuck in her story, was more than she thought she was, I realized that I too must be more than what my negative thoughts told me I was. And in that moment I surrendered to the fact that even though I had unknowingly spent years trying to fix my story, I couldn't. True, it was a part of me, but certainly it wasn't the whole me. Although I didn't have a clue as to what was beyond my story, I set out that day on a journey to understand why I had created this story and what purpose it served.

I spent the next ten years of my life examining not only my own story but the stories of others. While on this journey I learned three very important things: First, we create our life stories in our attempt to become someone or something. Second, our stories hold the key to our unique purpose in life and to its fulfillment. And third, hidden in the shadow of our story is a very special secret; once this secret is unveiled, we will stand in awe of the magnificence of our own humanity.

THE STORY, THE THEME, AND THE SHADOW

Our stories have a purpose. Even though they set our limitations, they also help us define who we are so we don't feel completely lost in the world. Living inside them is like being inside a clear capsule. The thin transparent walls act like a shell that traps us inside. Even though we have the ability to gaze outside and view the world around us, we stay safely trapped inside, comfortable with the familiar terrain, bound by an inner knowing that no matter what we do, think, or say, we can go no further. Our stories separate us and draw clear boundaries between ourselves, others, and the world. They limit our capabilities and shut down our possibilities. Our stories keep us apart even while we are begging to belong and fit in. They drain our vital energy, leaving us feeling tired, depleted, and hopeless. The predictability of our stories feeds our resignation and guarantees our fate. When we are living inside our stories, we engage in repetitive habits, abusive behaviors, and abrasive internal dialogues.

Like all good stories, our personal dramas always have a theme, which repeats itself over and over throughout our lives. We can decipher our unique themes by listening carefully to the conclusions we have made about the events of our lives. These conclusions shape our existence and drive our personalities. Our conclusions become our *shadow beliefs,* the unconscious beliefs that control our thoughts, words, and behaviors. Our shadow beliefs establish our limits. They tell us how much love, happiness, and success we are or are not worthy of. They shape our thought processes and define our personal boundaries. Disguising themselves as the truth, our shadow beliefs rob us of self-expression and squelch our dreams. But what's important to realize is that our shadow beliefs contain the very wisdom we need to transcend our current limitations and our discontent. They motivate us to compensate for our shortcomings and drive us to become the opposite of what we tell ourselves we are. Our shadow beliefs drive us to prove that we are worthy, that we are lovable, and that we are important. But, left unattended, these shadow beliefs turn on us, sabotaging the very things we most desire by letting their negative messages limit our lives.

WHY YOU "NEED" YOUR STORY

We stay wrapped in our stories—securely placed inside our capsules—so we can hold on to the comfort of what we know and rest in the safe and familiar feelings of being at home. When life gets difficult and we begin to confront the pain of our own limitations or the disappointment of living below our self-imposed standards, at least we can count on one thing: the predictability of our stories. Our stories give us something and someone to identify with. The worst feeling for a human being is to feel like a "nothing," that our lives and our individual existences don't matter. Most of us would much rather endure being an unlovable person than someone who is completely invisible. So, in a desperate attempt to give our lives meaning, we create and then repeat our stories; and as we cling to who we think we are, we perpetuate our dramas. Then, gradually and unwittingly, we actually become our dramas. We act out our stories and carry them around like badges of honor. We become invested in keeping our stories alive, and in the process we unknowingly become victims of the stories we created to protect our secret: We become victims of life.

When we recognize that we have identified ourselves with our stories and not with our broader, deeper, truer selves, our first impulse is to just get rid of the story. But because we have *become* our stories and have allowed them to dictate the scope and course of our lives, a scary question arises: If we aren't our stories, who are we? Outside our stories, life feels scary and uncontrollable. It reeks of unpredictability and uncertainty. We fear that if we let go of our dramas, we will lose our identities and whatever place we hold in the world. Who will protect us? Who will love us? To what will we belong? This is a devastating prospect for any human being. The unconscious fear that drives our stories is that if we surrender our identities, slow down, and go inside, we will be devoured by the emptiness. Our resistance to being nothing, to having nothing, and to being a nobody is at the very core of our human struggle. Our fear of nonexistence is so deep that most of us settle for a repackaged version of the self we know rather than wake up inside the unknown.

I spent most of my life struggling to be a "somebody," to have a purpose and a life of meaning. Yet over the years my spiritual search has taught me that in order for me to be free to be the special, unique woman that I am, I must embrace both the vastness of my Divinity and the insignificance of my humanity. I must embrace the fact that I am everything and nothing.

My rabbi, Moshe Levin, once told me a story that comes from the Talmud. A person is asked to write on a piece of paper the words *I am nothing but dust and ashes* and to place that piece of paper in his pocket and meditate upon it. He is then asked to write on another piece of paper the words *The entire Universe was created just for me* and to place it in his other pocket. As the seeker meditates on both realities at the same time, he realizes that both are true.

If we look at life from the largest perspective, we see that we are merely specks. Until we embrace our absolute nothingness and our own insignificance, we will forever be chasing the experience of being somebody. But once we surrender to the fact that we are *everything and nothing*—once we embrace both the story and beyond, the shadow and the light—we become whole, integrated human beings. We open ourselves up to a world beyond that which we know. We can then have the grand experience of seeing that we belong to and are a vital piece of the entire Universe. We will be able to marvel in the realization that the entire Universe was created just for us. Then we will grasp the enormity of our true essence.

I know that for some of you this may be a difficult concept, and you may not feel ready for it or comfortable with it yet. But I promise you that if you allow yourself to open up to this idea and explore it, a new possibility will arise. When you embrace both your wins and your losses, your frailties and your strengths, your vastness and your nothingness, you will feel safe enough to allow your Divine secret to emerge. Only by returning to the state of wholeness will you feel worthy and deserving of expressing the highest truth about yourself.

THE FALSE SELF

Our stories are like old friends. Even if they talk too much, at least we know what we are getting—an alternative that feels less threatening than connecting with a group of strangers. Most of us repeatedly choose the comfort of what we know, staying inside our limited realities, just so we don't have to face the terror of that which we don't know. But brewing beneath the surface is a deep discontent about the *false self* that we have created and the story that goes along with it. This is where the struggle begins. This discontent is always pushing us, whispering in our ears, "There has to be more than this."

In order to embrace the enormity of who we truly are and make the journey beyond our limited stories to find our true selves again, we first must face the ultimate truth and often the most painful reality: that we were never really separate from the Divine. We are a piece in a Divine puzzle. We may look separate, we may act separate, and most of us will go to our graves believing that we are separate, but our individuality is nothing but an illusion. It's a painful distraction that keeps us trapped in an endless chase for something more, better, or different than what we already have. And it's a futile chase, because it's based on the incorrect conclusion that we are somehow "flawed." In our separateness we struggle to create bigger and better versions of ourselves, trying desperately to fix what we believe is broken. We abandon our naturally Divine selves and frantically try to ground ourselves in our own unique identities. We forsake our Divine selves for our self-image. But that self-image—the identity we are chasing—is not who we are; it's the false self we've created to define ourselves. Our false self is the main character in our stories, and we mistakenly believe ourselves to be that person. It is our persona, the image we create to give ourselves a distinct identity. And our stories are our desperate attempts to make sense of our existence, to define what cannot be defined. Our stories are where our false selves reside. Our false selves are the heroes and the victims and the stars of our stories. They keep our stories intact and pacify us with a false sense of predictability and security.

SEPARATING FROM THE DIVINE

The moment we identify with our false selves, the moment we believe ourselves to be our stories, we fall out of the hands of the Divine and enter into the small illusion of "me," separate and alone. Then the game begins—the game of "Look at Me, I Am Separate from You." We engage in this charade because it allows us to hold on to the illusion that we are really separate and individual beings. Even if we intellectually understand by this point on our spiritual journey that we are all one, we continue, on an unconscious level, to fight for the separate life we are familiar with and to avoid the experience of oneness. We believe that if we face the ultimate truth—if we face our oneness—then that uniqueness we cling to will die. But facing that truth is our task, because living inside our stories and in the illusion of separateness is not really living. It's an endless game of wanting—fearing and wanting. It's a game you cannot win. It's a game of "If Only": *"If only* I were rich, famous, healthy, smarter, wiser, faster, shrewder, or younger, I would be able to win this game and find the happiness I deserve." *"If only* I knew more people, had a better job, or had my own business, I would have what I need and be happy." *"When* I get my new house, new car, new girlfriend, or some new clothes, I will feel so good." *"If only* I were appreciated, respected, loved, or seen, I would fulfill my deepest desires." Or maybe your game is about getting rid of something. *"If only* I weren't so selfish, fat, lazy, angry, bitter, tired, or broke." *"If only* my children, husband, or mother would stop acting out." Or, the big ones: "When I finally arrive at my perfect body weight or find my life purpose, I will be content."

This is an unwinnable game. It is a trap, an endless maze with no way out.

We work day and night trying to manipulate, strategize, and figure out ways to win the "If Only" game. But the game lives inside our stories. It was developed to keep us occupied and busy and give us a reference point for our individual identities. But if we are willing to look, we will see that the game is nothing more than a decoy, hiding what is real, covering up our true essence. To end this struggle we must see that much of what we believe about ourselves is a story. For most of us, it is a disempowering tale. We created our stories in order to give ourselves an identity and protect the sacredness of our true essence. And we will need our stories and the secret they hold to lead us back into the presence of our Divinity and to unfold the purpose of our lives.

EMBRACING YOUR STORY

Our stories have a Divine purpose. They are a real and necessary part of our personal evolutions. Until we understand the importance of our stories, we will stay trapped in the vicious cycle of trying to fix parts of ourselves that aren't broken. Hidden within our personal dramas is important information, pearls of wisdom for us to extract that hold the key to fulfilling our unique contributions to the world. Our stories contain the exact ingredients we need to become the people we always longed to be. Inside each of our stories is a Divine recipe for a most extraordinary life.

The first step in uncovering your recipe is to realize that you created your story not only to protect yourself but, unknowingly, to gather the wisdom and experiences that are necessary for you to realize your life's purpose. You created your story in order to learn the lessons it had to teach. You are like a master chef. You have spent your life in the kitchen, cooking up pain, joy, triumph, and failure in order to gather the ingredients necessary to manifest your most extraordinary self. But your story—with all its drama and all its unprocessed pain—conceals this recipe.

Most of us get so distracted by the drama of our stories that we no longer remember that we have a Divine purpose here. We are so committed to the pain of our personal histories and to making others wrong that we don't even realize that all of our pain has a purpose. This bears repeating: All of our pain has a purpose! It is here to teach us, guide us, and give us the wisdom we need to deliver our gifts to the world. Most of us use our traumas and our wounds to beat ourselves up, to stay stuck, and to keep ourselves small. But when our pain and disappointment are examined and used as learning tools, they impart sacred life lessons that can be taught to us only in this way.

You are here to contribute your own unique flavor and serve the world in a way that only you can. One of my son's kindergarten teachers, Mrs. Knight, demonstrated this principle to her class. On the first day of school, Mrs. Knight handed all the children who walked into class a piece of a jigsaw puzzle with a number on the back. As she called up each student by his or her number, each brought their piece of the puzzle and Mrs. Knight placed it in the correct position of the cardboard frame that held the puzzle together. There were twenty children and twenty pieces of the puzzle. When Mrs. Knight finally called number twenty you could see the entire picture on the puzzle except for one missing piece, which prevented all of us from seeing the beauty of the entire picture. The little boy who had received piece number nineteen was missing from class that day, and in order for the entire picture to be revealed, the class needed his contribution. Thus Mrs. Knight beautifully illustrated to the children how important each of them was to completing the whole.

I sat there with tears in my eyes thinking about how each and every one of us represents a vital contribution to the whole of humanity. Each of us has an important piece to contribute to the picture of life. When we are stuck in the past, hating our lives, our stories, and ourselves, it is impossible to claim our piece of the puzzle and put it in its destined place. Until we make peace with our stories, it's impossible for us to extract the ingredients we need to express our Divine selves. All of our drama—each of our experiences, the parts of ourselves that we love and the parts that we hate—is what makes our piece unique. Some of us got the middle piece of the puzzle, some the end, while others got the big round piece. There is no other piece of the puzzle just like yours. None. There are similar ones, but nothing like yours. Your unique contribution lies dormant, waiting for you to collect all the experiences you need to fulfill your piece of the puzzle. Every day you call forth experiences perfectly suited to gathering the wisdom required to produce your unique recipe, your piece of the puzzle.

THE PROCESS

The Secret of the Shadow will guide you to see that "the story of you" does not begin to define who you truly are. It's a small part of you that keeps you trapped in repetitive patterns and limits the amount of love, inner peace, and success you can receive. In order for you to see your whole self and to view your true magnificence, you must step outside your story. Stepping out of our stories allows us to let down the perfectly constructed walls that surround our open hearts. In order to live outside our stories, we must heal our wounds and make peace with our past. We must uncover the pain and embrace the flaws and inadequacies that come with our humanity. Until we come to terms with who we are and why we are here, and understand the tremendous lessons that life is teaching us, we will remain trapped inside the smallness of our own personal dramas.

In order to transcend your story, you must be willing to experience the daily struggle of your personal existence. For only when you can be with your life exactly as it is do you have the choice to change its direction. To live a life outside the confines of your story, you will first learn to clearly define all the ways you keep yourself separate, encapsulated in your story. You will develop the willingness to come to terms with all the ways you avoid acknowledging and accepting with love the nothingness that lies within you. You will learn all the ways you try to define yourself so that no one will mistake you for someone else, the ways you seek to fill up your identity so you won't have to feel the deep void, the emptiness, that lies beneath your wanting.

This book will show you how to use your story, to get value from all your traumas and shortcomings, to gain wisdom from your wounds. It will give you the process by which to extract your unique recipe and unleash the secret that lies hidden in the shadow of your story. Now is the time to explore how you can use your story to enrich your life and the lives of others. That's why you have it. But you will only be able to use it when you are ready to step outside the story called "You."

In the chapters that follow we'll identify all the endless ways we've chased fulfillment and happiness. Whenever we are blindly chasing something, we must stop to question why we are doing this; here is where we will find important clues. Whether we're chasing love, attention, respect, or worldly success, we must be willing to see that all our chasing is an attempt to fill some emptiness or lack that resides deep within our beings. We must acknowledge how our strategies to find fulfillment have failed. Then we can come face-to-face with all the ways we have violated ourselves, all the places we have sold our souls while trying to make ourselves and our stories better.

The Secret of the Shadow is about discovering your true essence. It will serve as a guide that will lead you back home—where, deep within, you know you belong. Standing in the presence of your true essence, unencumbered by your story, you will know yourself as the totality of the Universe—both the nothingness of your smallest self and the fullness of your humanity. Stepping outside your story, you will discover that the "you" you have always desired to be does not live inside your story. Once outside, you will see that the life of your dreams, and the fulfillment of your deepest desires, are waiting for you. Here you will feel compelled to share with the world the secret that has been hidden in the shadow of your story. Then you will know what it is like to stand in the glory of your most magnificent self.

HEALING ACTION STEPS

1. Begin by buying a beautiful journal, and title it, "The Great and Mysterious Story of Me." Commit to using this journal as a place to record the feelings, thoughts, and insights that arise as you do the exercises outlined in this book. As you do these exercises, try not to edit or censor yourself; instead, allow yourself to freely express whatever is on your mind or in your heart.

2. Choose a time when you can be alone, and make yourself comfortable. Create a space that is free from distractions, and have your journal nearby. Close your eyes, and as you do, take a few slow, deep breaths, feeling yourself go deeper inside with each breath. Allow yourself to relax completely, to fall still, and devote the next few minutes to your spiritual growth and self-discovery. Take another slow, deep breath, and allow your awareness to rest gently in the area of your heart. As you breathe, feel yourself connecting with your inner being—the essential aspect of you that has been with you every moment of your life.

Imagine that you are watching a movie of your life. See yourself on the day you were born; notice the faces of those who cared for you as an infant. Picture yourself in your early years, learning to walk and talk. Recall the years you spent in school, seeing the faces and hearing the voices of those who touched you—for better or for worse—during your formative years. Allow this movie to keep playing on the screen of your consciousness, and let yourself feel and remember your loves, losses, disappointments, challenges, and achievements. Trust that whatever is coming to your mind is perfect. Breathe deeply as you reflect on the many experiences you have had in the time you have been on this earth.

Consider that each of these experiences, and every one of your life's events, has unfolded in harmony with a Divine plan. Open up to the possibility that every person, event, and incident has been drawn into your life in order to awaken you to your own inner wisdom. Reflect on the idea that you have been born with a unique contribution to make and that every experience of your life has in some way been training you to deliver your special gift to the world. Take another deep breath, and when you are ready, slowly open your eyes and spend a few minutes journaling about whatever thoughts or feelings are present within you.

3. Each chapter of this book will include a contemplation—an idea to be savored, pondered, and taken in slowly. Take your time—a week, or even two—and reflect deeply on the words in each chapter's contemplation.

Contemplation

*"My life has
a Divine plan."*

Chapter 2

YOUR UNIQUE RECIPE

I n your life you have tasted the sweetness of love, the sour disappointment of loss, the bitterness that remains after too many heartbreaks. Every one of these experiences is part of your unique recipe. You wouldn't be you without them. These experiences, when integrated and understood, will give you everything you need—every bit of wisdom, insight, and strength—to live your ultimate dream.

The Universe in all its perfection conspires to give us exactly what we need to fulfill our recipe. It gives us all the happiness, all the unhappiness, the wanting, the fulfillment, the addiction, the aspirations, the trauma, the divorce. Think about the unique circumstances each of us was born into. Some of us were born African American, others Caucasian, Hispanic, Asian, or multiracial. Some of us were smothered, while others were neglected;

some of us were beaten, and some were coddled. Some of us were given everything, while others had nothing. We may think we got a bad lot in life, but we got the precise lot we needed to complete our recipe. Every experience of our life has contributed a distinct and essential ingredient to the recipe called "you."

Imagine that God is a master chef whose desire is to create millions of different desserts in order to please and delight his children. In his wisdom he knows that many different ingredients are necessary to make such a feast. He knows that a cake made only with sugar will not satisfy. So he gave us all the ingredients we would need to become the most delicious dessert we could be. Every experience of loss and gain, pleasure and pain, contributed an essential ingredient. Each of these ingredients is filled with wisdom, and exists to teach us, guide us, and deliver vital information that will support us in becoming the person we most desire to be.

THE RECIPE CALLED DEBBIE FORD

Inside the painful, dramatic story of me I found the perfect recipe to create the Debbie I longed to be. My list of ingredients began with being the youngest of three children, with a brother and sister who were not exactly excited to meet me. Mixed into my recipe was a desperate need to be liked and accepted, and an extremely sensitive emotional system. Add to that a noisy internal dialogue that constantly battered me, letting me know how unwanted and unlovable I was. Stir in thirteen years of drug abuse so I could learn the depths of my own darkness and develop a profound relationship with powerlessness. Blend in a little self-loathing and a massive dose of neurosis. Mix in a large amount of self-determination so I would be driven to devote five years of my life to searching for the answers to some of life's most difficult questions. Add in twenty-five years' experience in making every-thing and everyone wrong—God wrong, the Universe wrong, my parents wrong—so that I would know with certainty that I had the power to make myself miserable for the rest of my life. Finally, add a pinch of arrogance and a belief that I knew it all and you have the perfect recipe to motivate me to find the answers to how I could love and accept all parts of myself.

It took me many years to see that my mission to "fix" myself was an endless and thankless task, a bottomless pit leading me nowhere. I truly believed I would feel better once I got rid of the parts of my recipe I didn't like. But struggling unsuccessfully against the unwanted parts of me led me to discover that I didn't need to get rid of anything. Instead, I needed to integrate and embrace everything.

I realized that in order to be the "me" I always desired, I would need every ingredient that had gone into my batter. I would need every experience of weakness and strength, fear and courage, suc-cess and failure. As long as I kept trying to stick my hand in the batter and rip out certain unwanted ingredients—my trauma, my weakness, my self-doubt—I would remain an uncooked lump of potential. But if I integrated all my ingredients, mixed them up, and appreciated the unique contribution they made, I would finally be able to recognize that I had all the makings of the perfect me. I had spent years trying to become someone other than myself, so the realization that all I had to do was *stop* trying to be something

I wasn't was totally enlightening. I came to understand that in order to make the perfect cake you sometimes need a little salt, and that when you overcompensate for your batter's bitterness by adding heaps of sugar, your cake becomes indigestible.

Each of us comes into this world with a particular mission, as if a recipe for our highest fulfillment were written within our souls. This recipe is different for each of us; there are no two recipes that are exactly the same. To discover the recipe called you, you must distinguish what lies within your batter.

My recipe required me to wait thirty-eight years to find the perfect man to spend my life with. Then it called for me to give birth to my most favorite person in the entire Universe only to watch my marriage fall apart in front of me. The next ingredient was an unexpected divorce that kicked up all the trauma and pain from my own parents' divorce. The overwhelming fear that I couldn't make it on my own added some nice flavor so that I could muster up the courage and the strength to write my first book, *The Dark Side of the Light Chasers*. All those traumas—those ingredients—gave me the willingness and wisdom to dig down deep into my soul and produce that book.

In a million years I would never have guessed that all my pain and darkness, all my selfishness and my never-ending desire to make a difference in the world, were being carefully blended together so that I would be able to step into the highest version of myself. But the perfect recipe for my life was waiting to be discovered. I learned to trust in the powers that be and came to the humbling realization that no one really knows what experiences we need in order that we may give our greatest gift.

In doing what was necessary to heal my issues with my ex-husband, I was unknowingly gathering wisdom and essential ingredients to add to my recipe. Preparing to write my second book, *Spiritual Divorce,* forced me to grow and expand and take responsibility for my reality, no matter what my ex-husband—or anyone else, for that matter—was doing. It forced me to take the high road and ask, "How am I going to grow from this? How can I use this to make me my most Divine self?" Of course I had other options: I could have hated my pain; I could have felt sorry for myself because I had a lot of pain. Instead I chose to look for the gold, the jewels, and say, "Aah, why would I need this? What can I extract from this situation? What can I now contribute that I couldn't have if I had never had this experience?" I have lived the perfect life to do the work I do. Because I couldn't support others in healing their pain and creating the life of their dreams if I hadn't first done this for myself.

A DIVINE BUFFET

Imagine flipping through your favorite cookbook and seeing several recipes for *passionate, fulfilled, abundant, extraordinary human beings.* Intrigued, you quickly turn to the indicated pages to learn what ingredients would make up such masterpieces, and on the first page you see:

> Mix together fourteen traumas, four heartbreaks, a mother who loved too much, a father who was emotionally unavailable, and one cheating husband. Blend in the

opportunity to be a single mother with two children. Add four extra doses of selfishness, a shadow belief that says, "I'm not good enough," and an ego that screams, "I'm going to prove to everyone that I *am* good enough," and *voilà!* You have forty-two-year-old Lynda, a perfectly satisfied chief financial officer of a $17 million company!

Or try this one:

Combine divorced parents with twin brothers who badger you on a daily basis. Mix in four years of a bad marriage and one very successful business, six years of depression, and one immune deficiency disease. Add a noisy internal dialogue to remind you that there is definitely something wrong with you. Garnish with a deep inner knowing that things will work out if you suffer long enough. Add a passionate love of music and the arts, bake at high intensity for forty-three years, and *presto!* You have Jeffrey, a songwriter and producer of a children's TV show that teaches kids how to be kind to each other.

Or how about a taste of :

Start with two parents with high expectations and a need to control your every move. Add a heaping dose of inadequacy, twelve years of striving to be the perfect student, sixteen amazing victories, and sixteen experiences of deep emptiness. Add two suicide attempts and four opportunities to be brought to your knees. Sprinkle in a love for math and science and a knack for empathizing with people's problems. Add an unshakable faith in God and stir in one serving of self-realization. Chill for thirty-two years. Meet Pam, a pediatric psychologist with a holistic approach.

It's fairly easy to see how your positive attributes contribute to your unique recipe. You can probably appreciate how your talents, your natural abilities, and your childhood dreams have added to your life and to the person you've become. But the traumatic events in your life—the experiences that left wounds within you— are an equally important part of the mix that will help you become all that you can be. Every insecurity, every fear, every tragedy, every obsession, broken relationship, and shameful incident holds clues that are leading you toward your most magnificent self. Blend them together and they will propel you into the unique contribution that you are. If you embrace all the ingredients in your recipe and allow them to be part of your batter, what will come out of the oven is the person your soul longs to be.

USING YOUR INGREDIENTS

Most of us suffer endlessly from the painful and unwanted parts of our recipe, but there are some extraordinary people who choose to use their pain to contribute to the world. The death of a child is one of the worst ingredients anyone could imagine having in their recipe, but what if it was in the Divine plan for you to use that experience to save the lives of thousands of other children? John Walsh, the host of *America's Most Wanted,* did just that. After his six-year-old son, Adam, was murdered, John became an advocate for victims' rights and brought awareness to a subject that had for years been buried in the dark. Unwilling to allow his child to die in vain, John turned his anger into action and established a national program to incarcerate tens of thousands of criminals and sex offenders. John Walsh could just as easily have chosen to wallow in his grief for years, but instead he chose to use it to make a contribution to the world.

Identified as one of the most severely abused children in the state of California, Dave Pelzer was brutally beaten and starved by his emotionally unstable and alcoholic mother. Through his courage, strength, and forgiveness, Dave turned his wounds into wisdom and wrote a gripping account of his life's story, which touched the lives of millions. His book, *A Child Called "It,"* was a *New York Times* best-seller for three years and was nominated for a Pulitzer Prize. While few would consciously choose severe physical and emotional abuse as part of their life's recipe, we have to thank God that Dave chose to use his experience to make a profound difference in the lives of others.

When she was just nineteen months old, Helen Keller was rendered blind and deaf after suffering a nearly fatal fever. Rising above the ignorance of her time and her own frustration, Helen became determined to interact with the world using her remaining three senses. She became a skilled and passionate communicator and the author of thirteen books. Lecturing around the world in support of the handicapped and the underprivileged, she almost single-handedly destroyed age-old myths about blindness. Imagine what the world would have missed if Helen Keller had made the choice to immerse herself in self-pity, rejecting the ingredients in her unique recipe.

Viktor Frankl was imprisoned in Auschwitz for five years. After his mother, father, and pregnant wife were all killed by the Nazis, Frankl clung to what he called "the last of the human freedoms—to choose one's attitude in any given set of circumstances." Embracing the devastating ingredient of these deaths inspired Frankl to write *Man's Search for Meaning,* a book that has been recognized as among the most influential works of humanistic literature.

We need to be able to look at our entire history—including our traumas, handicaps, failures, and life circumstances—and say, "Thank you, God, for giving me that." Because these experiences were tailor-made to support us in delivering our unique contribution.

Just think about it. Why did some events wound you so deeply when they didn't matter at all to the rest of your family? Consider that you needed the wisdom that that incident had to offer. Maybe that pain held a huge lesson that you would have missed if it hadn't been so severe. Maybe you needed to be born with a devastating handicap so you could prove the indestructibility of your spirit. Maybe you needed to survive the devastating loss of your child so you could save thousands of others. Maybe you needed to bottom out on drugs, alcohol, or self-loathing before you could muster up the courage to take responsibility for your life. All of our traumas and emotional issues exist in order to support us in the unfolding of our highest selves. Many of our most important ingredients are hidden under a veil of pain. This pain is encoded with vital information and wisdom that we need to assemble our unique gifts. There is nobody who can teach what you can teach. There is nobody who can offer your unique perspective. Until you see the perfection of all your ingredients, you will constantly be trying to change, fix, and heal your story rather than using it for the Divine purpose for which it was intended.

THE PAIN OF HATING YOUR RECIPE

Most of us spend the majority of our lives judging the ingredients in our recipe—making what's inside us wrong. We say, "I have too many eggs" or "There's not enough sugar" or "If only I had more spice . . ." In other words, we reject some aspects of ourselves while we embrace others. For as long as she can remember, my girlfriend Shirley was told that she had a big mouth. She used to get into trouble at school for talking too much and felt like an outsider in her circle of friends because it wasn't cool to have so many opinions. Even her family was embarrassed by her outspokenness and cautioned her on more than one occasion to tone it down a bit. Shirley spent the first twenty-plus years of her life hating this ingredient in her recipe and tried unsuccessfully many times to get rid of it.

One day, while attending her favorite sociology class in college, Shirley was passionately speaking out as usual. After the class, her professor took Shirley aside and said, "You talk so much! Have you ever considered pursuing a career in radio? You could get paid to talk all day long!" Suddenly a light flashed in Shirley's mind and she saw a huge gift in this ingredient that she had always considered to be a curse. Shirley went on to create an award-winning radio show, and today she enjoys a rewarding career as an outspoken and well-loved radio talk-show host.

It is not an easy task to see the perfection of your wounds and inadequacies, but there are no accidents. You—and I mean all of you—are Divine. You might not be expressing the Divine in your current form, but I assure you that once you transform your emotional wounds you will see their perfection. Take horse manure, for example. If you went for a walk in the country and found a pile of manure on your path, you would probably cringe and back away. But to a master gardener interested in growing the biggest and best roses or adding vibrant color to a crunchy bell pepper, that same pile of manure would look like pure gold. What most of us call poop the gardener calls pure potential, because he recognizes it as just the ingredient he needs to nourish his garden.

Hating any part of our recipe guarantees that we will attract painful experiences into our lives. Like attracts like. Our unprocessed pain and self-loathing will call forth people and events that will reflect back to us how we feel about ourselves. Whether in the form of accidents, abusive relationships, financial ruin, or bad jobs, we will constantly find ways to beat ourselves up, because we carry a deep-seated belief that who we are is wrong or that what has happened to us is wrong. When we are unable to see the Divinity of our recipe we are doomed to a life of anger, disappointment, wanting, and longing. Our traumas, wounds, disappointments, and pain have come bearing gifts, but until they are integrated they will remain unprocessed lumps in our batter. When we extract the wisdom from these experiences, we find the unique ingredients for our recipe. We have all the qualities, the capabilities, the wisdom, the perfection, the imperfection, and the wherewithal that it takes to bring forth and give the gift that only we possess.

In metaphorical terms this process is about gathering, sifting, mixing, and blending the ingredients we already have in order to make the best dessert imaginable. In Universal terms it's about embracing and integrating each piece that has contributed to making us who we are today so that we can deliver our unique creation to the world. Accepting ourselves at the deepest level and offering our unique recipe to the Universe is the greatest feast of the human spirit.

Our dramas are an indestructible part of who we are. No matter what we do or how hard we try, we cannot get rid of them. The only choice we have to make is whether we are going to use them or they are going to use us. I've chosen to use my dramatic life story to write books, to contribute to others, and to earn a living. Maybe that was the master plan for me: suffer endlessly for twenty-six years and then learn from my past, heal the pain, and turn around and help others learn to transcend their suffering. Today I feel grateful for my pain, knowing that I could never teach what I teach without it. I thank God for the trash and trauma of my past; otherwise, half the pages of my books would be empty.

Look into your recipe, look into your story, and see what you are not accepting and blessing. This is a good place to begin. Until you see the necessity of owning *all* of who are, you can't extract the jewels from every experience of your life and your story will continue to use you. It will continue to clobber you over the head and make you act as though you're small. But the moment you see the value in the parts you hate as well as those you feel good about, the moment you recognize that painful event as the perfect ingredient to make your recipe complete, you will witness the magic of transformation. You will bless what you formerly saw as a curse. You will watch as the horrid becomes holy.

Remember, you can spend the next forty years trying to take ingredients out of your batter, or you can just stir it and allow all your trauma, victories, heartaches, and joys to blend into the Divine mix called you.

HEALING ACTION STEPS

1. Think back over your life, recalling the experiences that most profoundly shaped who you are today. Make a list of the significant victories, losses, joys, heartbreaks, and disappointments that have made your life distinct.

2. Make a list of the aspects of yourself and your life that you have had difficulty embracing—the parts of your recipe that you have tried to get rid of. Maybe you have long resisted the fact that you are not athletically inclined or the perception that you are less attractive than others. Have you felt cheated or defeated because of a handicap, a loss of love or money, or a trauma that occurred many years ago? Make a list of all the ingredients in your recipe that you believe have no value or have been a thorn in your side.

Contemplation

"Every aspect of me and my life contributes an essential ingredient that allows me to fulfill my Divine purpose."

Chapter 3

EXPLORING THE GREAT AND MYSTERIOUS STORY OF YOU

E ach of us has a story that is uniquely ours. Like a fingerprint, it distinguishes and separates us from those around us. Etched within our stories is the accumulation of everything that has left a mark on our lives. Every person, event, circumstance, and situation that has touched us deeply traces itself into our psyche. Whether our lives have been touched by a great parent, a childhood illness, an inspiring teacher, or a neglectful caregiver, each of these experiences remains with us, becoming an integral part of our identity. The conclusions we make about these events, as well as the meanings we assign to them, get ingrained into our psyche, creating the story line for our personal dramas.

I want to make sure you understand that your story is not bad. In fact, it is probably your most precious commodity. But it is vital for you to know that even though your story is not bad, it is limiting.

Your story encapsulates your existence, limiting it to a small, insignificant part of your humanity rather than allowing you access to your entire self. But as soon as you recognize your story, make peace with it, and extract its vital ingredients, you can step out of the smallness of your lowest thoughts and step into the fulfillment of your greatest dreams.

DISTINGUISHING YOUR STORY

Our stories contain the collection of feelings, beliefs, and conclusions that we have been accumulating and dragging around our entire lives. Our stories are heavy because they live inside our egos and our egos are almost *always* serious. They are seldom filled with light, love, and the frolicking delight of a child at play. Most often they are focused on the negative. The whole basis for our stories exists in what could have been, should have been, or might have been. Our stories are sprinkled with pain, loss, and regret and frosted over with hope, desire, and fantasy. Our dramas live in the memory of the past and in the fantasy of the future. Every negative thought about the past that enters our minds lives inside our stories, as do all our feelings of loss and hopelessness. Our fantasies about "The day this happens" or "When I finally reach my goal" live inside our stories. Rarely do our stories show up in the present moment, when we are simply being with what is. Like shadows, our stories follow us around wherever we go, hiding the truth of who we are. They are never far out of sight, but they can only be seen when they are examined in the light of day.

Recently I led a weekend workshop as part of a seven-month Integrative Coaching Program that I teach. The second night of the workshop we decided to have a pajama party. Sixty of us curled up in our favorite pj's and prepared for a fun-filled evening of "story time." I was wearing my favorite Mandarin Chinese pajamas, while others came clad in flannels, nightdresses, and housecoats. Some of the men sported oversize T-shirts and boxer shorts with cute little prints. Since our focus that evening was to be on distinguishing and sharing our individual personal dramas, I wanted to create a light and uplifting atmosphere to offset the seriousness that most of us attach to our stories. We take our stories so seriously, I explained, because we believe they are the truth.

The purpose of our pajama party was to explore and expose both our stories and the shadow beliefs that hold our dramas in place. I asked everyone to close their eyes and try to remember a time when they were small, before the age of five or six, when they felt lost, alone, sad, or scared—a time when something happened that jarred their reality. I asked them to notice whatever event came to mind and explained to them that this incident would, even though they might not understand its significance, hold a clue to the theme of their personal drama.

I shared with the group what came up for me the first time I did this process. The incident that popped into my mind was a scene in front of a house I lived in when I was three. I could see many people running around, looking behind bushes, and talking secretly to one another. I was standing by the side of the house, huddled in a corner next to the wall. Someone had just robbed a store in our neighborhood, and the police thought the man had run through our yard. My entire family and many of our neighbors were all excitingly looking for clues to help in capturing this criminal. I stood scared and separate from the crowd. No one seemed to notice me. I felt like I was caught in a world that I had no part in. All I could see through my young three-year-old eyes were a bunch of grown-ups not caring about where I was or what I was doing.

Unknowingly I had made a critical decision that day that would forever alter the way I perceived myself and others. I made this incident mean that no one cared about me. And like any good human, I had to come up with an explanation for *why* no one paid attention to me. I decided it had to be because I wasn't important enough to deserve their attention—because, after all, if I were important, my family and relatives would have noticed me and would have cared that I was feeling alone and ignored. Of course, I could have chosen any of a number of interpretations, but once I was inside my story I had to choose the most disempowering explanation I could find. It turns out, not surprisingly, that "No one cares about me" is one of my core shadow beliefs and is the central theme in my personal saga. Standing there more than thirty years later, I still remembered feeling completely left out and all alone.

After I shared this story, it became clear to the group what their assignment was for the evening. Everyone then set out on the mission to uncover their life drama, the story that defines who they are and keeps them locked inside the capsule of their individual realities. We split into smaller groups, huddling together in tight little circles, and began.

Peter, a soft-spoken man in his mid thirties, decided to go first in our group. He sat there, staring blank-faced at us. I asked him to close his eyes and recall an incident from his past. After a couple of moments, Peter began to describe a time when he was six years old. His mother had walked into his room while he was playing with his best friend, John, and, with anger in her voice, had begun to reprimand the boys for leaving their bikes on the front porch. When Peter didn't respond to her, she had flown off into a rage and begun screaming, smacking him, and telling him he was good for nothing and that she wished she had never had him. Peter had been traumatized. He sat drenched in his own tears. Peter decided that day that his mother's words and actions meant that he was bad and didn't deserve to be alive.

The humiliation from that event still showed on his face twenty-nine years later. It was obvious by the level of Peter's emotion and the clarity with which he recalled this event that he had touched on one of his core shadow beliefs: "I am good for nothing." Together with our group Peter began to look for the ways this theme had woven itself into the other events in his life. In a very short time Peter recounted numerous other events about his overbearing, abusive mother and the ways she confirmed his belief that he was in fact "good for nothing." He shared all the ways he had been dominated by her, how he felt powerless to stand up to her and be a man, and how, as a result, he had never learned to stand up to the women who came into his life.

Peter constantly found himself with women who would remind him that he wasn't good enough to be with them. Painfully he shared all the ways women had taken advantage of him, and how powerless he felt whenever he was in the presence of a woman he loved. Peter shared how he has been trying to prove that he is good for something by going out of his way in his personal relationships, and how he strives to be useful and helpful. But, he added, he always seems to fail. His story constantly confirms that his mother was right and that he is, in fact, "good for nothing."

Elizabeth, a shy girl and one of the youngest in our group, waited quietly for her turn and spoke only after I had reassured her it was okay. In a soft voice Elizabeth told us that she was an only child and that both her parents were highly educated professionals who always had high expectations of her. To the great disappointment of her parents, Elizabeth never did well in school. Even the best tutors couldn't help Elizabeth bring her grades up to par, and when she was seventeen she received the crushing news that she hadn't been accepted into the college her parents had chosen for her.

Elizabeth made that incident mean "There is something wrong with me," and this shadow belief became the theme of her life story. She felt like a failure and resigned herself to the fact that her life would never amount to anything. Since she had already decided she wasn't smart enough to win her parents' approval, she opted out of going to college and focused all her attention on getting married and starting a family. But after three years of trying to get pregnant, Elizabeth was told by doctors that she couldn't conceive a child. Again she was faced with the overwhelming feeling that there was "something wrong with her" and that she was a disappointment to her husband and to herself.

The stories went on and on. The more of them we heard, the clearer it became that each of us was living according to the shadow beliefs that had become the theme of our stories. We were spending our time creating events and situations that allowed us to act out the themes of our dramas. It didn't matter how much pain surrounded the stories or what we chose to make the events of our lives mean; one thing was universal: The story was always dramatic, repetitive, and highly personal. The major themes, although slightly different, all wept, "There is something wrong with me. I'm not good enough. My life doesn't matter." The common song was "Poor me, poor me, poor me."

As the night went on, we began to extract the shadow beliefs that infiltrated all our personal stories. Until that night most of the people sitting there had held these beliefs to be the truth rather than what they were: shadow beliefs that had become the main story line of their dramas. I explained that although each of us has many shadow beliefs, one of them will take on the central theme in our personal dramas: thus Peter's "I am good for nothing" theme, and Elizabeth's "There is something wrong with me." Over the last ten years I have led thousands of people through the Shadow Process, a three-day transformational workshop. And in doing so I have discovered that there are three main shadow beliefs shared by virtually every human being. These beliefs are:

I'm not good enough.

I don't matter.

There is something wrong with me.

I have also discovered that there are countless variations on these beliefs. As you read the list of shadow beliefs that follows, see if you can identify the core belief that serves as the theme of your story.

Nobody likes me.

I don't belong.

Something's wrong with me.

I'm too stupid.

I'm incompetent.

I'm unwanted.

I'm not enough.

I'm a doormat.

I'm not special.

I'm unworthy.

I'm undeserving.

I don't matter.

I'm unimportant.

I'm inappropriate.

I'm inadequate.

I'm insignificant.

I'm useless.

My life doesn't make a difference.

I'm a nobody.

I'm damaged.

I'm rotten.

I'm a mistake.

I'm bad.

I'm not okay.

I'm incomplete.

I'm flawed.

I'm unlovable.

I'm a failure.

No one cares about me.

I can't trust anyone.

When our shadow beliefs are triggered, they reinforce our stories, proving to us how "accurate" and "true" our dramas really are. Every thought we think triggers an emotional response in our bodies, and when we are living inside our stories we have access to a very restricted range of emotions. Here are some of the feelings that live inside our stories: resignation, lack, deprivation, resentment, victimization, loneliness, anger, blame, shame, despair, hopelessness, sadness, fear, guilt, jealousy, envy, regret, self-pity, and self-loathing. Each of us telling our stories that evening could see how these emotions had been our constant companions.

In the safety of our pajama party it was easy to see how small we had each chosen to make ourselves. Although there was some good in all our stories, in our group of sixty people there were few stories that screamed, "Look at me, look at how great I am!" or "Look at what an extraordinary human being I turned out to be!" There were few stories that were guided by love, compassion, or contentment. Even though many of the people in our group had accomplished amazing things and were highly regarded in their fields, our stories were not of bigness and greatness, but rather of the fear of a child who had bought into a lie about who they were and what they were capable of. What came out on that night was all our loss and despair, all that was lacking or missing in our lives. The consistent message that each of us gave off was "If only": If only we had different parents, lovers, friends, bodies, brains, or luck—if only we had had a better education or a more supportive family—we would be the people we most desired to be. All of us could see how we had given up our greatness and our power in some area of our lives in order to stay locked inside our stories.

All of us could see particular areas of our lives where our dramas played themselves out. Some of our stories revolved around our careers; others enacted our dramas on the stage of our relationships, families, or finances. Some of our dramas showed up in our emotional states or our physical bodies. Often our dramas overlapped into two or three areas of our lives. But the point that was made on that glorious night was that at some time in all of our lives we stepped out of the world of infinite possibility and stepped into the world of our own limited reality. This is where our troubles began and our limitations originated.

Many people could identify the story they had created as a child but had a difficult time seeing the impact of that story on their lives today. A few people shared that their lives were completely void of drama: Their story was that they didn't have any drama or any story. Donna, a clinical psychologist, said that she had a great life. She had two kids and a thriving practice and was perplexed at how the whole idea of the story related to her. I asked her to tell me a little about her life. She said, "I had a great mother and father, I had a good childhood, and everything is fine. In fact, I've always been the rock of our family, the one who everyone calls for reassurance. I've always been the voice of sanity." At that moment our eyes met and Donna heard her own words. They were, more or less, exactly the same words she had uttered thousands of times before to describe her life. They fell out of her mouth automatically. Stunned, Donna realized that she had just inadvertently uncovered the theme of her story: that "everything is fine." No matter what was going on in her life, she could always put a smile on her face, pull herself up by her bootstraps, and convince herself that everything was perfect.

It's important to note that not all stories are sad, traumatic, or painful. There are some stories whose theme is "Everything is great" or "Just perfect, thank you." But even those "happy" stories run out of fuel and carry heavy limitations. For Donna, living inside the story that "everything is fine" prevented her from taking any risks that might involve her seeing that life is not always perfect or happy. Her story kept her trapped within a safe but limited reality. Although she lived in the illusion of happiness, she sacrificed being bold, adventurous, and outrageous, and this stopped her from ever examining her deepest desires.

HEARING THE SONG OF YOUR STORY

"How can we tell when we are in our stories?" "How can we hear them?" These were the questions everyone wanted answered. A sure way to find out whether we are living inside our stories is to examine the quality of our thoughts and the internal dialogue we engage in on a daily basis. Many people spend most of their lives being somewhere other than where they are in the present moment. When they are at work they are thinking about being at home. When they are at home they are thinking about going on vacation. When they are with their children at the park they are thinking about watching their favorite show on television. Their bodies are present, but their minds are somewhere else. I know that I spent the first thirty years of my life somewhere besides where I was. I lived for the fantasies in my mind, dreaming about what might make me feel better, always trying to give happier endings to the aspects of my life that were not at all happy. I spent at least twenty years dreaming about the man of my dreams and how when I met him I would finally reach utopia.

Future gazing is a sure sign that we are deep inside our stories. When I wasn't dreaming about the future, I spent my time thinking about the past: all that went wrong, all that should have turned out another way. I could spend a week reliving an argument I had with somebody in a grocery store over who was first in line. When you're inside your story, the quality of your thoughts can range from fearful and morbid—like worrying about freak accidents or unlikely tragedies—to the trivial and the absurd, like obsessing about a button on your sweater or the neighbor's dog peeing on your lawn.

When we are in our stories, we never think a thought just once. We don't think, "I would love to have a great relationship" and leave it at that. We think, "Oh, I hope he comes soon. I hope he doesn't have an ex-wife. I hope he is kind and loving and will buy me a ring. I hope he doesn't burp out loud or stink up the bathroom." We might dream about lying on the beach in Hawaii, looking better than we've looked in ten years and having passionate, fulfilling sex. Then we think, "I hope he doesn't hurt me. I hope he's not like that last lying jackass." And then we think about the last creep we had a relationship with, and off we go on a tangent about how badly we've been wronged and how much better we would be doing if we hadn't ever gotten involved with that person. Inside our stories we rethink the same thoughts over and over—future, past, future, past, future, past, past, past. . . . It goes on and on and on. It's tireless. When we live inside the smallness of our individual stories, it is often so painful that the only way our minds can deal with the pain is to daydream or dwell in the past.

MEETING YOUR SHADOW BOX

All this internal dialogue goes on inside what I call the *Shadow Box,* the container that holds the ongoing, never-ending internal dialogue that lives in our minds. Imagine the loudest boom box that ever disturbed your peaceful time at the beach. Now put that inside your head. This will give you a sense of the disturbing noise of your Shadow Box. Your Shadow Box is filled with every thought you've ever suppressed—all your judgments, all your righteousness, all your unprocessed emotional wounds, and all your shadow beliefs. Your negative internal dialogue is like psychic indigestion. Until you digest all the unconscious thoughts and feelings that live within your psyche, you will continue to live in the noise and discomfort of your Shadow Box. Stop for a moment and listen to the thoughts in your mind. Now allow your attention to drift onto a project that isn't getting done or a relationship that is not working out. Now listen again. By this time you should be clear about what your Shadow Box is.

Our Shadow Boxes live inside our stories and go with us wherever we go. They constantly whisper to us all our flaws, all our disappointments, and all our inadequacies. Our Shadow Boxes let us know what we really think about ourselves while we are inside our stories. While our intuition tries desperately to get our attention, more often than not we turn away, pledging our allegiance to our Shadow Box, that familiar voice that loves to remind us of our failures, our inadequacies, and our self-imposed limitations.

A couple of years ago I gave a lecture to one hundred people in the ballroom of a large hotel. When we began, everyone was comfortably spread out around the room. Then suddenly the fire alarm went off. A loud voice came over the loudspeaker, and a repeating taped message began: "This is the fire marshal. The fire alarm has been engaged. Please go to the exit door closest to you. You must exit immediately. This recording will not be turned off until you leave the building." Since this was the third time the alarm had gone off that day, no one in the room was too concerned. The ballroom was on the ground floor, and we were sure we would be able to flee if in fact there was a fire.

At that point we had only forty-five minutes left together, and we decided to gather closely on one side of the room so we could hear each other speak and so I could finish my lecture. As the fire marshal's message repeated itself over and over, I had to raise my voice so everyone could hear me. Even though they were more interested in what I was saying than in what the recorded message was repeating, they couldn't help but be distracted. Then the thought occurred to me that this recording was a splendid example of our torturous internal dialogues. I asked the group, "How many of you would choose to listen to this tape all day long for the rest of your lives? How many of you would buy a little box that repeated this recording and listen to it while you work, while you're out on dates, or when you're watching a movie? Would any of you deliberately buy a box like this and carry it with you wherever you go, clutching onto it for dear life?" Of course, they all said no.

I stayed quiet for a few minutes so my audience could once again listen to the tape recording repeat its all-important message. Then, looking deeply into their eyes, I asked, "How many of you spend more than an hour a day listening to the internal chatter that goes on and on inside your head?" Everyone sat quiet, getting a glimmer of what I was talking about. Everyone could see that every day they wasted a large part of their precious energy listening to the repetitive tape that plays over and over inside their minds, saying things like, "That wasn't very good. That wasn't very smart. You shouldn't have said that. What is she talking about? Why don't they just turn off that recording now?" Or it might be babbling on with, "I didn't pay all this money to come to a lecture and listen to this alarm all day. I wish she'd just get to the point." Or maybe you wake up next to your husband and in your mind you hear, "Why doesn't he brush his teeth before he has his coffee? If he would just earn more money I wouldn't have to work so hard." Maybe your Shadow Box spits out things like, "No one cares what I think. I'm so alone, no one wants to be my friend." Or maybe you didn't finish yesterday's project on time and your Shadow Box thoughtfully reminds you, "Look what you did this time. You really blew it, you're just like your father." But what is most disturbing is that no matter how many times you've heard it before, you *still* listen. You listen again and again, actually taking that voice seriously.

How many of you have spent thousands of hours listening to that box in your mind? Maybe you have even avoided going to a party or having fun in some other way so you could stay home and listen to that box. Some of you have stopped yourself from pursuing a better position or going back to graduate school, basing your actions solely on the feedback you've received from your charming little Shadow Box. Someone suggested I invent a Shadow Box: For $14.95, I will program your internal dialogue so you can listen to it every day. You can carry it with you wherever you go. Or it can act as a talking alarm clock. You just turn it on in the morning and it says, "Good morning. God, you look awful today." That way you don't even have to say it yourself. Your Shadow Box will say, "Nothing worthwhile is going to happen to you. You don't have what it takes. It's never going to get better than this. You might as well stay in bed today, because no one notices you anyway." You may be up for a raise, but your Shadow Box will scream, "It's never going to happen for you! It's not fair. They don't really appreciate you. Life is tough. What do you know? You're a loser. You're never going to make it." Or "Poor me, why can't I get a break? Maybe I can win the lottery this week. Then I'll be happy." Or if you're on a roll and things are going great, your lovely little companion will chime in, "If you get too big, people won't like you. You can't have it all. Don't get too big for your britches."

I felt excited and lucky to have had this experience of the fire alarm, because most people never understand that their internal dialogue is like a bad tape that plays over and over, unconsciously, without edit. Most of us choose to listen to that voice every day. Most of us listen so intently that we can't even hear what the people around us are saying. The Shadow Box talks with certainty, and if you begin to ignore it, it will say, "No, listen. This is important. Nobody likes you. No, *really,* they don't like you." Or "You're never going to amount to anything. Really, you're just a loser." That's how your Shadow Box sucks you in. Every time you buy in to your Shadow Box, you are buying in to your story.

To grasp the repetitive nature of your Shadow Box, you might try recording your internal dialogue for a month or so. Then you can look back and say, "Oh, I've heard this conversation before! Look, on February 4, 1999, I heard it, and on April 14, 1998, 1984, 1981 . . . I heard it forty-two times this year, sixty-four times the year before . . ." How many hours a day do you think you spend listening to that Shadow Box, analyzing it, bargaining with it? It's like a maze. You think there are actually some cookies at the end of that tunnel. You think that if you listen to it long enough you're going to get some reward. But this is the *big lie*. There are no cookies at the end of that tunnel, and you will not be rewarded if you listen to it long enough. However, your Shadow Box does act as an alarm. The alarm's recording is saying, "This is a recording. You are living inside the story called 'You.' If you wish to turn this alarm off you must take the giant step outside your story. Once you are outside, this recording will automatically shut off. Thank you for listening, and have a beautiful day."

Long after the hotel's fire alarm had been disabled we sat laughing at our Shadow Boxes, which had now been taken out of the shadow of our consciousness and spread out like a giant buffet of inner dialogues to be viewed by the entire group. Everyone could see how protective they felt about their Shadow Boxes, as if exposing their negative chatter constituted some sort of grand betrayal. Most people could see that they held their inner dialogue as unique and special. No one dared admit how similar the messages of their Shadow Boxes were to those of the people sitting around them. Most of us, if not all, had spent a good portion of our lives trying to quiet our Shadow Boxes, and as far as we could tell, all of us had failed. We had tried pacifying them, bargaining with them, and manipulating them. Some had tried suppressing and drugging them—anything to shut them up so that we could finally be free to enjoy our lives, so that we could step outside the never-ending, predictable stories of ourselves.

Chances are you have spent years striving to alter, rework, correct, adjust, and fix your story, unaware that you have any other choice. My goal is to offer you another choice, one that rests on the understanding that you are not your stories—any of them. I want you to see that although you have many stories, many shadow beliefs, and an overly talkative Shadow Box, all of these come bearing great gifts—gifts intended to propel you outside your story and into the greatest expression of yourself. All of them are there for you to learn from and then to use to deliver your unique contribution to the world. I promise you that the life you are striving for lies beyond what you know and far beyond the limitations of your story.

HEALING ACTION STEPS

1. Write the story of your life in all its dramatic detail. Give special emphasis to what didn't work out and to what could have, should have, or would have been better. Allow yourself the freedom to be completely candid about your failures, losses, disappointments, and regrets as well as your hopes, desires, and dreams. Give voice to the thoughts, feelings, and beliefs that live inside your story.

2. Read through your personal drama and see if you can begin to distinguish a particular theme. Is there an underlying pattern that has replayed itself over and over throughout the events of your life? Do you frequently wind up feeling left out, abandoned, betrayed, disrespected, unseen, or taken advantage of? What is the distinctive flavor of your "poor me" story?

3. To unconceal the shadow beliefs that drive your personal drama, make a list of the conclusions you have formed from your life's events and the meanings you have assigned to those events. Read over the personal story you wrote for the first step listed here, and as you reflect on each significant event of your life, ask yourself, "What did I make that mean about me?" It may help you to look over the list of shadow beliefs presented earlier in this chapter. See if you can distinguish your top three shadow beliefs. This will help you to uncover the theme of your story.

4. Dedicate some pages in your journal to writing down the repetitive internal dialogue that is broadcast from your Shadow Box. Notice without judgment the conversation of your story.

Contemplation

*"The deeper truth
is that I have a story
but I am not my story."*

Chapter 4

WHY YOU HOLD ON
TO YOUR STORY

O ur fear of change, our fear of stepping into new realities, is so deep that we desperately cling to the world we know. We often mistake familiarity for safety. The perceived comfort we derive from what is familiar keeps us living in the illusion of our stories. But the question we should ponder is, Are we really safe inside our stories? Instead of risking change, we hold on for dear life and resist the uncertainty of the unknown. I once read a story about a woman swimming across a lake with a rock in her hand. As this woman neared the center of the lake, she started to sink from the weight of the stone. "Drop the rock," shouted some people who were watching from the shore. But the woman kept swimming, now disappearing for moments at a time under the water. "Drop the rock!" the onlookers hollered louder. The woman had reached the middle of the lake and was now sinking as much as she was swimming. Once more the people urged, "Drop the rock!" And as the woman disappeared from sight for the last time, they heard her say, "I can't. It's mine."

Most of us have spent too much time resisting our dramas rather than looking for the wisdom in each of our unwanted aspects, beliefs, and circumstances. Resistance locks us inside the emotional pain of a situation. It traps us in the reality that we most want to change. Resistance comes from wishing or wanting our present circumstances to be different. Even the slightest desire for things to change can create massive amounts of internal resistance. Whether we are resisting our entire story or just a small piece of it, resistance causes us internal imbalance. It acts like glue, attaching us to the very feelings and beliefs we most want to shake free from. Even though it might seem backward, the first thing we need to do in order to heal is to accept all that we have been resisting. For the last seven years, in over fifty different cities, I have repeated these words: *What you resist persists.* If you take the meaning of this phrase to heart, you will have the power to make permanent, healthy changes in all areas of your life. Even though I continually teach people to embrace all that they are, most people insist on hating or disliking some aspect of their lives. It doesn't matter which part of their lives it shows up in—their bodies, their relationships, their parents, or their finances—resistance and healing do not go together. So if you choose to resist anything in your life—if you hate it, judge it, dislike it—you have guaranteed that the issue will persist.

Resistance denies us inner tranquillity and the happy ending we so desire. It is the reason we stay the same. Resistance to going beyond and moving through our issues is the cause of our repetitive behaviors. Resistance to *what is* sucks our vital energy and blocks the natural flow of our evolution.

THE COST OF RESISTANCE

Our resistance is triggered whenever we make ourselves, others, or the world wrong. The internal belief that sets up our resistance says, "It shouldn't be like this." We then spend all our energy trying to change the reality of our circumstances. When I lecture, I love asking people, "How many of you have spent more than one thousand hours of your life trying to change the people around you, the events of your past, or some quality about yourself that you don't like—whether it's your fear, your selfishness, your fat, or your bank account?" Everyone, and I mean everyone, raises their hands. Most of us believe that if we resist the unwanted conditions of our lives long enough or hard enough, they will go away. One thing I can promise you with absolute certainty is that resisting *what is* will never make it go away. It might drive you deeper into denial and deeper into your story, but it won't change what happened to you when you were three, it won't help you lose twenty pounds, and it won't make you like your ex-husband.

In my studies of karate, my teacher taught me that sometimes the best way out of a compromising situation is to let go. For example, if an attacker grabs my arm, instead of tightening up and pulling away I need to step toward my opponent and relax my arm completely. Pulling away from my attacker triggers a natural response in him to hold on tighter. So in order for me to get away from my attacker I must first surrender to his grip. When I let go and relax, my opponent's grip will naturally loosen, giving me the opportunity to break free from his hold. Our initial response is always to resist any perceived threat. Yet it's only when we breathe deep, relax, and lean into the experience that we stand strong and gain access to all our power and strength.

In order to transcend our suffering, we must go against our instinct to hold on and instead surrender to the path of letting go. Anything we want to change, anything we're afraid of, anything that we are angry about or refuse to accept will keep us glued to the past and attached to our stories and the shadow beliefs that drive them. Surrendering to *what is* requires us to soften our hearts, let go of the expectations that come out of our stories, and accept whatever life presents us. Surrendering to all the ingredients that have made up our lives invites us to listen with innocent ears to the deeper message of our pain rather than being stopped by the familiar con-clusions voiced by our Shadow Boxes. Only when we admit that we are clinging to the comfort of our stories will we be able to soften our resistance and gain the wisdom of our life's experiences. Only by making a new decision to use our stories to love ourselves rather than to beat ourselves up will we ever be free to use them in the way they were designed to be used. I promise you that if you let go, if you resign as General Manager of the Universe and as the star of your drama, your life will get easier and you will be able to hear the deeper calling of your soul.

NOBODY'S COMING

There is no better time to begin the process of seeing your story for what it is, with all its limitations and its promises, than right now. There is no one who can do this for you. Nobody is coming to save you. For me, the tides changed when I came to this unsettling realization. For years I kept trying to make my life better. I worked hard to change the circumstances of my life, but I always seemed to fall short of my desired results. Then one day, sitting on the bathroom floor of my apartment and feeling sorry for myself, a light went on and I had a profound and life-changing realization: No one was coming. I could continue to suffer, to work hard and try to make my story nice and fun filled and easy like I dreamed of, or I could get off the floor, grow up, and face the fact that no one was coming to save me. In a moment of grace I realized that I had waited my entire life for my mother, my father, or the man of my dreams to come pick me up and tell me I was perfect, that my life was perfect, that I could have anything I wanted, and to promise me that from now on we would have a fairy-tale existence.

Unknowingly most of us are waiting for someone or something to rescue us. But I am here to tell you, no one is coming—not your mother, not your father, not a prince on a white horse. Though most of us think that if we wait long enough someone will step in and save us, the very sad truth is that nobody can travel our path for us. If we are brave enough to give up the hope that anyone is coming to save us, we will take an important step toward taking responsibility for our lives and our happiness.

STEPPING INTO HOPELESSNESS

Most of us spend a lot of time fooling ourselves into believing the good old "One day soon I will catch up with my dreams" story and enrolling ourselves in the hope that our lives will get better. Even though we need hope in times of great distress, it is important that we distinguish between authentic hope and wishful thinking. Often we trick ourselves into believing we are getting somewhere when really we are getting nowhere. Hope, positive thinking, and pleasant fantasies can easily turn into denial. Several years ago I was involved in a very stressful relationship with a boyfriend. I had spent years hoping it would get better. My hope prevented me from taking responsibility for my own feelings and dealing with the problems at hand. Instead of spending my time looking at my options and learning the lessons that were being presented to me, I spent hour upon hour daydreaming—wishing and hoping that one day, miraculously, everything would be okay. Instead of dealing with reality and going into the pain of recognizing that I'd had yet another failed relationship, I sank into denial—or, if you prefer acronyms, DENIAL (Don't Even Notice I Am Lying). My perceived hope had put blinders on my eyes and plugs in my ears, which served only to delay the inevitable. Reality is often painful. The great paradox and irony of it all is that if we are willing to give up the hope that we can change, fix, or transform our stories, if we are willing to let go and feel the hopelessness of no longer knowing who we are, we will find hope again.

I have found so often in my coaching practice that people would rather hold on to a grain of hope than deal with reality. Our fear of dealing with loss or pain keeps us tied to our stories and keeps us repeating the same old, same old. Some people get their fix of hope from books, tapes, and lectures. While this type of inspiration can at times be useful, if we use it to justify our current circumstances it will become no more than just another page in our stories. Several years ago I worked with Margaret, a wealthy woman who at first glance appeared to have it all. Margaret traveled all over the world visiting spas and retreat centers and had the means to afford the best advice money could buy. A self-proclaimed self-help junkie, Margaret went from workshop to workshop hoping that spending time with people she considered to be important would give her the recognition she craved. But inside, plagued by insecurity, she felt unseen and unimportant. A seemingly insignificant incident like someone not returning her call would cause her to obsess for days. Margaret spent most of her energy searching for something that would make her feel like she belonged.

During our third session I noticed that Margaret seemed to be getting weaker: Her body was breaking down, and she appeared more frantic and fearful. I suggested that she detach herself from all the groups and individuals she had been clinging to in the hope that she would one day belong. Knowing that what she sought could be found only inside herself, I gave her the assignment to withdraw from her self-help addiction and turn her attention inward. But Margaret couldn't do it. She was too terrified of being alone, of being without all the distractions that held the promise of recognition and belonging. She continued in her familiar pattern of behavior, clinging to the hope that one day it would pay off.

Margaret read book after book, searching for a philosophy that would justify her actions, all the while gathering evidence that supported her in staying the same. Whenever I spoke to her about the self-destructive patterns she was displaying, she would quote a line from the latest book she was reading: "Debbie, I just read a book that says we are all doing the best we can. I'm doing the best I can, too." Margaret was very creative at coming up with ways to justify her behavior. One week she came in and told me she had been mistreated and verbally abused by her family. When I asked her what she wanted to do about it, she replied, "Everything's perfect exactly the way it is." I watched as Margaret continued on her painful quest, all the while grasping at the affirmations that held the promise of hope. She was more committed to the path of justification than to exploring the underlying issues that were haunting her.

I asked Margaret to make a list of all the expressions and inspirational messages she used in order to avoid dealing with reality. This was a person who had read every self-help book that hit the best-seller list and attended every seminar that offered any promise of happiness. In her search she had gathered quite a collection of aphorisms that kept her from feeling the desperation of her situation. Here are some of the pearls of wisdom she used to feed herself hope: "It's always darkest just before the dawn." "What doesn't kill me will make me stronger." "No pain, no gain." "There's a reason for everything." "God doesn't give me anything I can't handle." "It's a process." "Miracles can happen." "The Universe is working through me." "Let go and let God." "It's all an illusion." "This too shall pass." "There's always someone worse off than me." "Maintain an attitude of gratitude." "Do what you love and the money will follow." "Things always work out for the best." "What is, is, and what's not, is not." "Every cloud has a silver lining." "The joy is in the journey." "There's gold in the dark." "Time heals all wounds." "Today is the first day of the rest of my life."

All this wisdom, which Margaret had spent years of her life collecting, had now become just another part of her story, just another attempt that didn't work. Even though it's been three years since we worked together, when I run into Margaret in town she still gives me poetic excuses for why things aren't going her way and why she's stuck. Because she is unwilling to face the underlying problems that keep her addicted to certain people and organizations, Margaret remains stuck in the same repetitive patterns she knows so well. She has convinced herself that this is the way God wants her life to be, and that if the Universe wanted more for her, somehow the doors would magically fly open. Instead of going inside herself and asking, "Is there something in me that is causing the same things to show up over and over again?" Margaret continues to cling desperately to hope, leaving everyone around her with the hopelessness of her life.

I tell you Margaret's story as a word of caution. If you've been stuck in a bad situation or a disempowering relationship for more than a year, do not allow your story to seduce you into thinking, "It will all work out for the best." Because that is, after all, just another story.

71

THE GREAT ATTEMPT

Many of us have fallen into the never-ending trap of trying to fix our stories. Some of us have spent years of our lives and too much of our energy rewriting the plot or recasting the characters of our personal dramas, hoping to transform our lives and put our Shadow Boxes to rest. But no matter how hard we try to fix our stories, we continually wind up flattened by the limitations that our personal dramas hold in place. Although making some minor improvements will help us look and feel better, those moments of joy are short-lived. Unless we make the conscious decision to step outside the limitations of our stories, the temporary sense of freedom we feel after reading an inspirational book or listening to a motivational tape will be replaced by hopelessness and despair. Until we understand that the root of our problem is the mistaken belief that we *are* our stories, even the best Band-Aid is bound to fail.

Recently, I met a beautiful young woman at one of my courses. I immediately noticed Caroline's bouncy walk and cheerful personality. On all the breaks she walked by me, waited to get my attention, and then flashed me a big, beautiful smile. But by the second day of the process Caroline's smile slowly began to fade and was replaced by a look of sadness, fear, and despair. Finally she approached me, asking if she could have a few minutes of my time. She asked me if I thought this seminar could really help her and began sobbing as she told me how many approaches she had tried in an effort to find lasting peace. She had tried to keep a positive attitude, and when that failed she had gone into therapy. She had been to many personal-growth seminars, read hundreds of self-help books, and listened to countless hours of motivational audio-tapes. She now found herself devastated because after all those years of trying to fix herself she still felt a huge sadness just beneath the surface of her consciousness.

I asked Caroline to close her eyes and describe to me her life's most painful incident. She told me that when she was five years old her father had come home, picked up her older brother, and then left. Caroline didn't see either of them again for ten years. I asked her how she had dealt with the pain of that trauma, and she said her mother had told her that she had to think positive and keep a smile on her face. By the time Caroline was fifteen she was in so much pain that she began exploring every approach—from physical exercise to spiritual practices—that might offer some relief. She kept looking for a quick fix, some bit of motivation or inspiration that she could hold on to for a day or a week. But the relief never lasted long; eventually she would slip back into the hopelessness of her story. I gently suggested to Caroline that she use the weekend to grieve the loss of her brother and her father. She stared at me blankly. "You mean, go *into* the pain?" she asked.

I drove home that night thinking about all the years each of us spends trying to change our stories, trying to pretend that our traumas or humiliations never happened, and trying to conceal the pain of our past. I reflected on the massive amount of energy we each expend trying to change the way we feel, the way we think, and the way we behave—all in the hope that one day, with enough work, our lives will transform themselves and we will finally be happy.

Every time I lead a seminar, I have the privilege of sitting in front of a group of some of the most extraordinary people on the planet. These are people who have worked hard at their lives. Some have studied with the greatest spiritual masters of our time; others have worked with therapists and other wise teachers to heal their pasts and make a contribution to the world. Yet still they are left with the feeling that there is more for them to know, more wisdom to be attained, before they will be whole. Their lives are driven by an internal struggle that continually keeps them searching for a better, ultimately more meaningful, life. For years I questioned why none of us can seem to find whatever it is we are looking for. Why, with all this knowledge, with all this wisdom, are we still on the hunt for something more? Why do bad things happen to good people? Why is continuous joy so unattainable? Why do our dreams always seem to be one step ahead of us? Some of us have even driven ourselves deeply into debt looking for the answers to why our lives are the way they are.

In one of my trainings we listed all the methods, techniques, and approaches we had used to try to fix ourselves and our stories. The list was huge. We had visited acupuncturists, past-life regressionists, and, for most of us, more than our fair share of therapists. We had worked on our anger, our inner child, and our inner critic, and when that failed we had tried ecstatic dance. We had tried visualizing, affirming, chanting, and meditating our way out of our pain. We had sought the advice of nutritionists, trainers, life coaches, yoga teachers, and gurus, and when those didn't work we had sought out our internists for a prescription of Prozac. We had cleansed our chakras, sniffed essential oils, and lit scented candles to calm our minds. Some of us had soaked in energetically balanced baths while listening to harmonically soothing music. We had burned incense specially imported from India, put magnets under our pillows, worn amulets around our necks and mood rings on our fingers. We had picked angel cards and had our tarot cards read. We had tried volunteering our time, doing service to help people who seemed worse off than we were. Some of us had tried a rich husband or a young, pretty wife.

Our list went on and on, and even though we had a tremendous laugh over it, most of us were left in the presence and pain of the story that couldn't be fixed. And the question that arose was simple: Is there any hope?

GOING BEYOND THE KNOWN

A deep longing drives us to fix our stories. We long to return to our natural state of wholeness, to the place where we know we are the vastness of the Universe rather than the smallness of our personal dramas. In our effort to find utopia, the land of peace and fulfillment, we form relationships, build businesses, and attend retreats. We spend hundreds of hours reading, studying, and accumulating knowledge that we hope will return us to our natural state of grace. But even when our knowledge fails us we continue our search. Deep inside we know that a return to wholeness is possible. After all, if we truly believed it was unattainable, we wouldn't spend so much of our lives chasing it; we would settle instead for the repetitive drama we all know so well. But most of us don't settle. That deep longing drives us to find our way home. It drives us to search until we wake up to the vastness of our eternal self, the self that is beyond our story.

When we are ready to remain conscious inside our stories, we must confront our deepest truth: *Our minds can't take us where our hearts long to go.* Our minds drive us to find answers, but the answers we find are often what prevent us from finding our deeper truth. For example, our society knows more about dieting and health than ever before, yet our population continues to suffer from health and weight problems. Knowing what to eat and knowing how much exercise we need *will not* give us the motivation to eat well and exercise. However, if we get in touch with the sacredness and wholeness of our inner beings and feel what it is like to be healthy and strong, we will naturally desire to feed ourselves and take care of ourselves in the best way possible. My friend Patrick says, "Knowing the way is not going the way." Knowing is the booby prize. Knowing lives in our minds; being lives in our hearts. In order to be the "you" that you long to be, you must give up the "you" that you know. In fact, you must give up all that you know. I am constantly amazed at all the men and women who walk into my seminars who can literally recite the texts of some of the greatest spiritual books of our times. Yet they are keenly aware that, even with all this knowledge, with all this wisdom, there is still something missing.

THE FEAR OF LETTING GO

Holding on to what we know is the biggest reason we remain stuck in our stories. As humans, we desperately want to believe we know who we are. But thinking that we know who we are and what we're made of is actually what seals us inside our stories. Our thoughts are limited; they live inside the identity that we believe ourselves to be. Each of us has an ego that desperately wants to know. The ego doesn't want to know just for the sake of knowing; it wants to know so it can feel superior to the next person. This is the way of all human beings. It's not bad; it's not wrong. It's just what is. Don't spend your time trying to get rid of your ego; you can't. Just like you can't get rid of your story. They are essential aspects of your Divine recipe, which we will explore later on. But for now you must admit who is running the show and what motives are operating at all times in your life.

Our need to know, our need to control, our need to be right, and our need to be *somebody* are what keep us trapped inside our stories. It's a natural response to try to fix something that doesn't work, and if we can't fix it, our next impulse is to get rid of it. But no matter what we do, we cannot fix or get rid of our stories. If we did succeed in getting rid of our stories, we would never find out who we are at the deepest level. If we win the game of fixing our stories, we lose the bigger game of knowing ourselves, because we might choose to stay in our stories, convincing ourselves that ours is not really a story but rather who we are. If we do this, we will miss our opportunity to contribute our unique piece to the grand puzzle of life. It's like winning a fight but losing the war. What we think we will receive by fixing our stories pales in comparison to what we will win when we step outside our stories into the fullness of who we truly are.

Many of us are afraid to let go of our stories even when they no longer serve us, for fear that we won't know ourselves without them. "Who would I be without my story?" we ask. "I'm scared I won't know myself." I say hooray that you won't know yourself! It is so exciting not to know yourself. The self you know is a limited part—a tiny speck—of who you really are. It is like a single pane in a huge kaleidoscope filled with thousands of colors. You have been committed to thinking of yourself as one pane of crystal-red glass, when in actuality you are a thousand jubilant colors, all intertwined and dancing together to create magical images. Every time you turn the kaleidoscope in a different way, a whole new world opens up to you. By shifting your focus, suddenly you can see things you never saw before. The perspective you hold about yourself is nothing more than a limited view of your true nature.

HEALING ACTION STEPS

1. Create a quiet environment free from distractions. Take out your journal and free-write your response to the following questions:

Who would I be without my story?

What am I afraid I will lose if I give up my story?

2. Make a list of all the things you've done in an attempt to fix or get rid of your story.

3. Make a list of all the ways resistance shows up in your life. What behaviors, emotions, and beliefs do you hold that prevent you from accepting what is?

4. Make a list of all the ways you use hope to avoid dealing with reality. If there was no hope of a miracle happening, what changes would you make in your life today?

Contemplation

"It's safe for me
to let go of my story."

Chapter 5

RECLAIMING YOUR POWER

If I could make a difference in just one human issue, it would be to relieve everyone of the unbearable suffering of being a victim. The problem with this desire, of course, is that I don't have the power to relieve anyone of anything, including being a victim. Only you can relieve yourself. Everyone I've ever met has some story about how they have been victimized. Most of us blame our shortcomings on our parents, while others blame our teachers, our ex-husbands or wives, our perpetrators, our religious leaders, our friends, or our grandparents. Many of us feel we've been abused in our jobs, taken advantage of by our families, abandoned by God, or victimized by life in general.

The story of victimization tells us that somewhere along the road we have been wronged and that the crimes perpetrated against us are the cause of our pain. This is a story that will limit us and strip us of our personal power for as long as we believe it. Most of us have gathered strong evidence to validate our perception that we are victims of life. And this is certainly one way for us to look at life. If we view our lives from the perspective that we are not the co-creators of our realities, we *have* been wronged. But if we change our perspective, we find a bigger, more powerful reality that tells us *we* are the co-creators of our own experience. Viewing our lives from this new perspective, we can embrace everything that has happened to us as exactly what we needed in order to blossom into our full potential and move forward in our lives.

Victim consciousness is frightening, because when we are in it we don't always know we are there. Victim consciousness is such an integral part of our stories that we can't even see how deeply it affects our lives. Even if we don't feel like victims in the outer world, many of us have become victims of our own self-abuse. Instead of projecting our blame onto others, we turn it around and project it onto ourselves. Some of us think it makes us better people if we beat ourselves up rather than lay blame on those around us. If we prefer to blame ourselves, we probably have feelings of righteousness about those who prefer to blame others. But either way we are the victims: Either we are the victims of someone else or we are the victims of ourselves. Either way we are left powerless, and when we feel that way we are driven deeper into our stories. What a choice! Either someone else is beating us up or we are beating ourselves up. Either way we're left wounded. Either way we lose.

THE COST OF BLAME

As long as we are getting something out of our stories, we can never step outside of them. Without even realizing it, most of us get a huge payoff from making others wrong. There is an inner satisfaction that comes from pointing our fingers and assigning blame. Many of us will go to our graves blaming others for the condition of our lives. We will do anything to avoid taking responsibility for our part in our dramas. But making others wrong and holding on to the pain of our past means committing ourselves to a lifetime of limitation and misery. And as long as we are blaming others for our circumstances we have no freedom, because our resentment keeps us bound to the very people—and the very circumstances—we dislike. As long as we carry that seed of resentment in our hearts we will have to create some kind of pain, drama, or discontent in our lives in order to keep our blame alive. Most of us have a strong internal commitment to saying, "Look what you did to me." No matter how much we scramble in the outer world to make our lives great, this internal commitment to making others wrong will ultimately prevail. It will drive our behavior and draw forth the experiences to prove ourselves right: that we have been wronged, and that somehow that wrong has damaged our ability to manifest the results we desire. As long as we are committed to being the victims of someone else, we will have to find some way to sabotage ourselves in order to justify our resentment.

The only way out of this trap is to take responsibility. At the deepest level many of us avoid taking total and complete responsibility for the events of our lives. We do this because in taking responsibility we often feel like we are letting someone off the hook who has harmed us. But in truth, taking responsibility is the only way we can let ourselves off the hook. If a person victimizes us and we wind up becoming the greatest human being who ever lived, we will naturally give up making that person wrong and will no longer need or desire to rub the crime in that person's face. In fact, we will see how the skills we've developed and the pain we've endured have been a necessary part of our process.

I met Jerri, an attractive woman in her mid fifties, at a friend's house. As we talked, I learned that Jerri is a highly successful financial consultant. When I asked her what person or event had contributed most to her success, Jerri looked me straight in the eye and said, "My alcoholic mother." Intrigued by her answer, I questioned her further. "What did your alcoholic mother teach you about financial management?" I asked. Jerri told me that after her father left the family when she was a teenager, her mother became very irresponsible with money, frequently spending all the family's monthly income on a few wild nights on the town. In order to make sure that she and her two younger brothers had school supplies, clothes to wear, and food to eat, Jerri intercepted her mother's bimonthly disability checks and used the money to buy necessities for the family. "It sounds like you've had a knack for financial planning your whole life," I said to Jerri. "Not at all," she replied. "When I was younger, all I wanted to do was find a man to support me so I could stay home and raise a family. I wanted nothing to do with managing our finances. Then, when my ex-husband and I divorced, I was forced to make a living on my own.

"Faced with the challenge of starting a new career so late in my life, I looked to see what skills or abilities I had that would be valuable to others. It was then that I realized I had a knack for managing money and that it was because of my financially unstable childhood that I had acquired those skills. I decided to go back to school to get my CPA certification, and suddenly I realized that my mother had actually taught me a lot. Something shifted inside me when I had that realization. I was able to let go of the anger I had carried toward her, and no longer blamed her for being financially irresponsible.

"When I finally let go of blaming my mother, I could see very clearly the direction my life was supposed to take. From that point on it was clear that I no longer needed to suffer around my finances and could contribute my gifts to others while reaping the benefits of my success."

FORGIVING YOUR PARENTS

Taking responsibility is a process that often comes in layers. I have known people who came to the difficult realization that even after twelve years of therapy and countless transformational seminars they were still blaming their parents for their lot in life. Not wanting to feel as though they had wasted all that time and money, they adopted a spiritual approach that told them they had to take responsibility for their reality. Instead of exploring their deep-seated resentment toward their parents, they tried to make their stories better by saying things like "My parents did the best they could with the awareness they had. They were carrying their own heavy load. It's not fair to blame them." Though these statements might be true, it's important for people in this situation to really take the time to heal the issues from their past by finding the blessings in these events and not just making up new stories about them. Taking responsibility in the spiritual world has become a new form of self-abuse; it leaves us still locked into the victimization of our stories. It's another thing we use to beat ourselves up, to make ourselves wrong and disempower ourselves. This is just another, subtler form of victimization. It turns our outward fury into inward seething.

Taking true responsibility is a process, and it is the only way out of the victim story. It means acknowledging that we are co-creators of the dramas we have lived. Taking responsibility requires us to extract wisdom from our life experiences and find the gifts they hold for us, as Jerri did. It means learning the sometimes painful lessons that each experience has to teach us. Responsibility is our ultimate destination, but if we are harboring deep-seated resentments toward others, we must search them out and deal with them. Otherwise they will continue to poison our psyches, sabotage our self-worth, and suck the life out of our dreams.

There are many layers of healing when it comes to our parents. We can feel free at one time, and then something happens and we uncover another level of pain. But if we are not thriving in our lives, it means we are still carrying a little bit of "Look what you did to me" regarding our parents. Resentment is very deep. It can take a lifetime to peel off. But if we don't acknowledge that we have it, we'll never make the progress we desire. If we are continually blocked or stuck and can't find satisfaction in our lives, it means we are still carrying resentment. We might want to consider that in actuality we are withholding ourselves from greatness so we can justify our blame. Once we have completely forgiven our parents for their flaws and shortcomings, the best gift we can give them is to lead extraordinary lives, to shine as brightly as possible. But if we still have some resentment toward our parents or caregivers, we will unconsciously get back at them by being miserable.

Ever since she was a young girl, Lori had a dream of becoming an actress. Her teachers recognized her gift for self-expression and drama and encouraged her to pursue a career on stage. Lori's mother, however, was less than supportive. A proud and proper woman, Lori's mother had wanted her to go to a good college and find a respectable and responsible career, as her older brothers had done. After some thought, Lori ignored what she considered to be her mother's rigid opinions, and chose not to go to college. But she always resented her mother deeply for not encouraging her to follow her passion.

A year later, when Lori was nineteen, she became pregnant out of wedlock. It was 1965, she was living in a conservative Midwest town, and Lori thought the best thing she could do was get married. Because of her proper upbringing, it was important to Lori to feel like a dignified woman having a baby rather than feeling the shame of being a single mother raising a child alone. So Lori chose to marry someone she didn't love, knowing that in all likelihood she would end up raising her child by herself. It turned out that Lori was right. Just months after her son Joshua was born, Lori's husband moved out. Then, when Joshua was six months old, Lori's mother sent her a newspaper clipping announcing an open casting call for a new play that was coming to town. The play called for a leading lady in her early twenties, and her mother suggested that she should try out for the role. Lori was startled by her mother's sudden encouragement of her acting career, and began resenting all the times her mother had discouraged her from chasing her dream and put her down for having the desire to act. "Screw you!" Lori screamed as she tore up the newspaper clipping. In that moment, Lori made her mother wrong, decided never to act again, and sealed in her fate.

Blame and resentment are the toxic emotions that keep us stuck inside the smallness of our stories. Woven throughout our personal dramas is an underlying conversation that might sound like this: "Look what you did to me. You screwed up my life. I'm a nothing just like you"; or "I'm never going to amount to anything—just like you told me." We hold others responsible for our deficiencies and then set out to prove that we have in fact been ill treated and wronged. Our "poor me" story becomes our evidence, proving that we've been mistreated, neglected, or abused. And every time we fall short of doing our best, we have the perfect alibi. We get to say, "If I hadn't had that angry father, lousy girlfriend, alcoholic mother, or been raped, molested, beaten, ignored, abandoned, called names, I wouldn't be like this!" Then we use every failure, every disappointment, every broken relationship or botched business deal to support our conviction that we have been victimized. We continually sabotage our efforts toward success and happiness in order to hold on to our resentment and keep our stories intact. Our continued failures or misery prove to us that we are right and those we blame are wrong.

It's important to start to identify the people in our lives we get to make wrong by not living the life of our dreams. Maybe it's our mom, our dad, our stepfather, the nuns and priests who raised us, our rabbi, our guru, our doctor, the kindergarten teacher who didn't pick us. Maybe we get to make our sister wrong: If she hadn't done that to us when we were six, we wouldn't be such a mess. Maybe it's the bullies who made fun of us or the kids in our class who left us out. The people we blame offer a perfect excuse for our self-sabotage. We are unconsciously punishing them by not being as successful or as happy as we could be. We say, either verbally or nonverbally, "Look, I really am a failure. You really did hurt me."

I met Sunny, an aspiring writer, at a recent seminar. As we talked, Sunny told me that from the moment she was born, she felt that nothing she did was ever good enough for her dad. This was the theme of her story. The third of three daughters, Sunny was raised in a rural cattle-ranching town and was taught by her dad to work the farm as a cattle hand. Sunny was a sensitive little girl who was naturally nurturing and caring, but she didn't have the heart or the knack for ranching. Sunny told me how she used to run off the farm in tears after being asked to push a pill down a cow's throat or saw the horns off a baby calf. She was always left with the feeling of being worthless in her father's eyes. She wasn't the little boy she felt her father wanted her to be.

I soon learned that for years Sunny had been yearning to write a book about the lessons women teach one another. When I asked her what was holding her back from beginning the project, she said, "I feel in my heart that my book will be a national best-seller, and that when my dad sees me on the talk shows and opens the paper to find my name in print, he will go to church on Sunday morning and tell people, 'Look what my little girl did.' I never want to be so successful that he gets to claim part of my glory for his own." Sunny has wasted years of her life holding herself back from fulfilling her heart's desire just so she could deprive her dad of the pleasure of bragging about her.

By the end of the weekend Sunny could see how much of her power she has given away to her father. She could also see that had it not been for her father's disapproval, she never would have felt drawn to writing. I am certain that on the day Sunny fulfills her dream of becoming an author, she will thank God that her father was emotionally unavailable, because this lack of intimacy with him is what gave Sunny her dream. She will thank God for every little thing that happened to her, including the fact that he, with all his flaws, was her father. Sunny has a choice: She can choose to carry that grudge for the rest of her life, thereby depriving her dad of the right to be proud of her. But if she deprives him of her success, she also deprives herself. And she deprives the world of hearing what she has to say.

Most of us have been carrying around the same grudges our entire lives. And if we want, we can carry them around until we're eighty-two. It might feel good to blame our mothers or fathers, our sisters or brothers. Pointing our fingers at others feels good sometimes. It's a way of taking the pressure off ourselves. "You did it to me" feels a lot better than "I did it to me." But the questions to ask ourselves now are, How many years have I been making my mother or my father wrong? How many times have I repeated the same unhealthy behaviors in an attempt to make them pay? How many more years do I want to do this? What have I sacrificed by holding on to my grudges?

If we're not creating everything we want in our lives, we are probably holding resentment toward someone or something. If we're not fulfilling all of our desires, we are sabotaging ourselves somewhere. We are still more committed to *not having it all* than to being happy. If we start fulfilling every desire we have, there will be nobody to make wrong, and without that tie to our past we will be free to live the life of our dreams. When we have let go of our right to be a victim, we will understand that we had the perfect parents who taught us the perfect lessons. We will no longer resent them, no matter how much they misled or mistreated us. Released from the smallness that being a victim ensures, we will stand tall in all our power and all our glory, and we will be grateful for every single incident, both dark and light.

WHAT'S YOUR EXCUSE?

Whenever we are making others wrong, we are using them as our excuse not to live our lives to the fullest. As human beings we are masters at inventing excuses to justify the condition of our lives. Like a leopard blends into the surrounding jungle, our excuses camouflage themselves as truth. They hide out and whisper quietly in our ears every time we try to go beyond the boundaries of our story. The scary part is that most of us hold our justifications as truths rather than as excuses. In order for us to break free from our stories, we must be willing to expose the excuses we use to hold our stories together. With a discerning eye we need to look at our daily dramas, go through our list of reasons and alibis, and ask, "Is this the truth, or is it just an excuse?"

In order to begin the life-changing process of dismantling our current reality, we must expose the excuses we use to hold ourselves back and to stop ourselves from manifesting all that we want in life. Our excuses act like invisible containers surrounding us, setting the boundaries of where we can go and what we can achieve. Our excuses justify the condition of our lives while making us believe we are powerless to reach the unreachable and attain the unattainable. Imagine being surrounded by a clear glass container. Every time we wish to go beyond this invisible boundary we bump up against the glass and slide back to the place where we began. This is what happens when we believe our excuses. Unknowingly we continue to wind up back where we began, because our limitations have been set. They have been programmed deep into our minds, and like any good operating system they are just following instructions. Excuses keep us stuck in our current realities and perpetuate the continuous cycle of our discontent.

Our excuses can take many forms:

"It's never going to happen for me." "I can't have it all." "I'm not good enough, old enough, smart enough." Or how about "I'm too old, too stupid, too fat, too tired, too *[fill in the blank]*"? Does "I'm blocked. I'm stuck. I'm confused. I can't help it" or "I don't know how" ring a bell? How about "I'm too lazy. I don't have enough energy. I'm a procrastinator" or "It will happen in God's time, not mine"? Maybe your excuse is "I need more education, more information, or more help." Does "I'm not ready, I'll do it tomorrow, I'll never be ready" sound familiar? How about "If only I had a different childhood. If only I had a good role model. It's his fault, it's her fault, if he would just change, if she would just change. I don't have what it takes. Someone else could definitely do it better"? Is powerlessness familiar? What about "I need help" or "If I speak my mind, people won't like me" or "If I fulfill my highest potential, I'll be all alone. Haven't I done enough already"? How do your excuses sound?

Our personal dramas—our pain, our complaints, and our discontent—often become our excuse for not manifesting our most magnificent selves. Our dramas take up so much space in our lives that most of us wouldn't know ourselves without them. In order to disengage from our dramas and step beyond our limited perspectives, we need to see what we get out of holding on to them.

A quick process you can use to see if you are making an excuse is to ask yourself the following questions.

1. Is this the truth, or is this an excuse that I have heard before?

2. Would [name a person you admire and respect] see this as the truth or as an excuse?

3. Am I responsible for this choice, or am I making others, God, or life responsible?

Asking yourself this series of questions should help you to determine if you are justifying the condition of your life by making excuses. Let me give you an example. One of my favorite excuses used to be that I was too busy to have fun and take time off. I would hear myself constantly complaining as I told my dramatic story about how much work I had to do. Then one day my girlfriend Danielle cornered me and asked, "Debbie, who is in charge of making your schedule?" Although I knew that I was the one who was in charge of my schedule, I had a thousand excuses for why I had to stay so busy: "It's my publisher's fault. It's my sister's fault. It's my publicist's fault. It's my staff's fault. They need me." All of these excuses left me feeling powerless and like a huge victim. Unquestioningly, I accepted these excuses as the truth. Then I stopped and asked myself, "Is this the truth, or is this an excuse I've heard before?" My answer was, clearly, "I have heard this too many times before." Then I thought about my friend Cheryl and asked myself, "Would she see this as the truth or as an excuse?" I knew immediately that Cheryl would support me in seeing that no one in the world could make my well-being a priority but me and that I was using other people as an excuse not to take responsibility for my time. Next I asked myself, "Am I making others, God, or life responsible for my circumstances?" My answer? "Absolutely." It was then that I realized that all my reasons were just some form of an excuse that left me feeling like a powerless victim of my own life. I realized that if I wanted to have more fun and leisure in my life, all I needed to do was stop making excuses and take responsibility for my choices. And so I did.

Recently, while giving a lecture on excuses for participants in one of my coaching programs, I had yet another opportunity to examine where I might be using excuses in my life. I felt sure that

I had blasted through most of what had held me back and kept me repeating familiar patterns, but I looked anyway. Then, a week into my inquiry, I began to feel a cold coming on. My cold symptoms always seemed to be the same—a scratchy throat and a tired body. I knew those feelings all too well. It seemed I was always catching some kind of cold that would stop me in my tracks and land me in bed for a few days. Sometimes I would try to stop it from coming on by filling my body with every known supplement, and at other times I would just surrender to it and allow myself to be sick and stay at home. This particular week was an exceptionally busy one, and I felt I couldn't afford to be sick. In the middle of my usual regimen of taking vitamin C and astragalus, I had a startling realization: Getting a cold was my excuse. I was blown away. Suddenly the lights went on and I could see clearly that every time I needed rest—every time I had too much on my plate or too many commitments to keep—I would get a cold. This was my excuse, my reason, my alibi—my way of letting everyone know I was out of commission and couldn't take on any more. Most of all, though, catching a cold served as a billboard that said, "Don't expect anything more of me." Looking back at my childhood, I could see that I had a pattern of getting sick, and that that was how I received extra attention from my parents.

I went to bed that evening in awe of my realization, but still feeling like I was coming down with something. As I lay in bed I made a list of all the things I could do to take care of myself instead of getting sick. Closing my eyes and taking a few minutes to go inside, I was easily able to access the answers: What I needed to do was make sure I had plenty of time for myself every week. My inner wisdom told me very specifically that I needed to schedule at least one hour each day for nothing but prayer and meditation. In addition, I needed to schedule one day a month, a "Debbie Day," for doing things that nurture my well-being.

What I have noticed is that when I am not using my excuses and running myself ragged but instead following my inner guidance, I stay relatively healthy and strong. Many times now I feel like I am coming down with something, but by realizing that getting sick is just my excuse for giving myself attention, I can choose to take the time to give myself the attention I need, even if that means canceling plans and disappointing people. Giving up our excuses propels us into the powerful consciousness of taking responsibility for our lives.

When we take responsibility, we step into the full power of our humanity. We leave behind the limits set by our stories and push beyond our shadow beliefs, those beliefs that tell us, "You can't." We step into the potent knowledge that we can co-create our desires and our dreams. Taking responsibility for everything we are is the greatest gift we can give ourselves, because it makes us whole. It empowers us and supports us as we move toward our full potential.

Close your eyes and breathe into this thought: *At this moment I have the innate power to change the direction of my life.* Do you feel strong or weak? There is nothing more exciting for us than to know that we have the power to change. We get to choose how we want to view the world. Either we are inspired by the possibility of being the co-creators of every event in our lives or we remain victimized by our shadow beliefs, which drain our power, telling us that we don't deserve to have it all.

Even if you've been living inside the story that life has done it to you, when you can say, "I'm doing it to me," you will have the power to stop it or do it differently. The voice of power says, "I'm doing it. I created it. I'm responsible for it. I can change it." The voice of powerlessness says, "I can't help it. They did it to me. I can't get out of it." At each and every moment in your life you have the opportunity to choose which world you live in. This is your opportunity to define your world.

Powerful . . . . Powerless . . . . You choose.

HEALING ACTION STEPS

1. Make a list of all the areas in your life where you are experiencing limitation or frustration or where you are not receiving everything you desire. Now close your eyes, breathe deep into your heart, and give yourself permission to be completely honest. With your eyes still closed, ask yourself the following questions, recording in your journal whatever emerges.

Whom do I blame for the condition of my life?

Whom am I getting back at every time I fall short of manifesting my full potential?

What behaviors, addictions, or self-destructive patterns do I use to prove that I have been wronged or mistreated?

What payoff do I receive for making others responsible for my reality? What do I get to pretend, deny, or avoid?

2. On another piece of paper, make a list of all the excuses you use for why you can't fulfill your heart's desires. When you are finished, read your list of excuses out loud. Then close your eyes and go inside. Take some deep breaths and ask yourself the following questions, journaling afterward about any insights you receive.

How many years have I been using these excuses?

What is the need that my excuses fulfill?

If I let go of my excuses, what feelings and experiences would I have access to that are not available to me now?

Contemplation

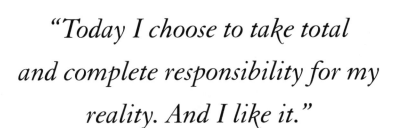

"Today I choose to take total and complete responsibility for my reality. And I like it."

Chapter 6

THE POWER OF PROCESS

We will stay in our stories until we extract all the lessons and wisdom we need in order to deliver our unique contribution to the world. It's important for us to understand that we created our stories—with all their magnificence and all their despair—in order to learn the particular lessons we need most. Our stories contain all the wisdom we need to become the people we long to be. The lessons for each of us are different. As Deepak Chopra so beautifully says, "We've walked through different gardens, we've cried at different funerals and we've knelt at different graves." Each of us has had different triumphs and failures, and has different lessons to learn. But Divine guidance has been instrumental in every experience of our lives, showing us ever more clearly who we are and giving us exactly what we need to fulfill our unique purpose. Our life stories have equipped each of us with a particular set of skills and a unique blend of wisdom that we are meant to deliver to the world.

To live outside our stories, we must courageously walk through our drama-ridden lives and begin the process of embracing and loving all that we are and all that we are not. We must take the time to examine each and every chapter of our lives, exposing the places where we are still stuck, hurt, or incomplete. We must commit to letting go of our resentments and to stop blaming others for the condition of our lives. We must be willing to take responsibility for our current circumstances and to let go of all the baggage we are still carrying around from our past. We must commit to traveling the path through our personal dramas and to finally making peace with our stories.

STOP CHASING THE FEEL-GOOD MOMENTS

Millions of people have spent billions of dollars trying to gain deeper levels of inner peace—to no avail. Others have been able to make some progress in feeling better about their lives, cleaning up their thoughts, their closets, and their relationships. Still others continue to search, trying desperately to find the right answer—the one that will free them from their suffering. But there is no way out. By avoiding our pain, we perpetuate our ongoing dramas and drag our past around with us every day. It is almost impossible to appreciate where we are or what we are doing when the past is right under the surface of our consciousness, stalking our every move, reminding us of our failures and our traumas. To begin the process of making peace with our stories, we must make a commitment to letting go of all the behaviors we use to anesthetize our pain. If we look closely at those behaviors and are willing to tell the truth, we will probably see that most of the ways we numb ourselves don't work very well anyway. In order for us to heal, we must stop chasing what I call the "feel-good moments." The following process offers you a way out of the never-ending cycle of discontent. It's not the easy road. I don't believe there *is* an easy road. But I promise you that the direct road to lasting peace and contentment is much easier to travel than the winding road of continually searching, trying, and failing.

Living a life where we feel that deep at our core there is something wrong with us—that we're not good enough or that we don't matter—is a hell that is difficult to endure. So is living a life in which our dreams are always one step ahead of us. The hopelessness, the discontent, and the seemingly endless pit of emotional pain kill our spirits and separate us from our most extraordinary selves. Nothing is worse for the human spirit. Nothing can take away our life force more than the belief that we are deficient or flawed, or that at some fundamental level we are unfixable.

EMBRACING IT ALL

The process of making peace with our stories requires us to identify, understand, accept, and embrace everything in our past that has caused us pain. The process is the same whether we are trying to heal a painful incident, integrate a shadow belief, or come to terms with an unwanted aspect of ourselves. Whether we suffer from depression, ill health, discontent, a sense of unworthiness, arrogance, or low self-esteem, the road to healing is the same. We process growing up with an angry mother in the same way we process being sexually abused by a cousin. We process the disappointment of losing a job in the same way we process anger at the person who breaks our heart. One might be more painful, one might leave deeper scars, but the path to healing remains the same. As we make the inner journey of embracing our story and all its ingredients, we begin to see the life that lies ahead of us, a life that will give us the gift of our eternal selves. Our traumas and failures, once they are understood and processed, will take us deep inside and return us to our Divine essence.

FINDING THE GIFT INSIDE THE PAIN

The issues that remain just beneath the surface of our consciousness are the lumps in our batter. These unhealed wounds are what prevent us from stepping outside the limitations of who we think we are. They are also the glue that holds our story in place. These lumps might seem inconsequential, but often they are linked to much deeper issues. For example, when I was in my early twenties I really wanted to be athletic. I admired people who played tennis, went skiing, and participated in other sporting events. Many of my friends and family members were great athletes, but I had the shadow belief that I was too skinny and weak to participate. Then I became interested in a man named Kevin, a professional tennis player. While we were talking one day, Kevin asked me why I didn't play tennis like my brother and sister. Immediately I launched into my story about how I was never encouraged to play tennis because I didn't have the right kind of body. I was told I wasn't strong enough or coordinated enough and that it would be more difficult for me because I was left-handed. With a quizzical look on his face, Kevin asked me how old I was when I was told these things. I tried to remember when I first heard those words. I saw an image of myself as a ten-year-old girl who felt awkward in her body. I could still feel the familiar sense of inadequacy and the shame of not fitting in. Fighting back the tears of this emotional wound, I shared with Kevin all the times I sat on the sidelines believing there was something physically wrong with me. Those painful memories had haunted me for years, keeping me from ever trying new sports or even playing volleyball at the beach. Kevin listened attentively and then, with a flirtatious gleam in his eye, said, "It doesn't look like there's anything wrong with you now. Why don't we go out and hit some balls?" My first impulse was to say no, but after a few days of encouragement I went out with him and hit my first tennis ball. To my great surprise, it came naturally. I committed to taking tennis lessons and have been play-ing tennis ever since.

By confronting this lump in my batter, this emotional wound that told me I was uncoordinated and defective, I broke through the limitations of that story. This one incident triggered a thou-sand other memories of times when I felt too thin and fragile. It allowed me to view all the times when I wished I had been shorter, fatter, and stronger. Confronting this unhealed emotional wound unraveled all the pain I experienced as a young woman who felt like a skinny little beanpole. I even cried through the pain of what I considered the most humiliating experience of my life: I was at my seventh-grade dance, wearing a burgundy velvet dress that my Aunt Laura had made me, when Todd Halpren, a popular boy at my school, picked me up and put me on the stage as the band's vocalist sang out: "Who's that girl with the skinny legs?" I was overwhelmed with shame and never wanted to set foot in that school again.

My skinniness was my deepest horror. I even tried to hide it by wearing two pairs of shorts or two pairs of pants. I spent hours in front of the mirror, trying unsuccessfully to make my body look different. The truth be told, all throughout my adolescence I thought of myself as Olive Oyle with big hair. And yes, I did wear my hair big for many years, thinking it would trick others into believing I was bigger than I was. For years I tortured myself, believing that if only I had a different body I would fit in and be okay. As I now processed this lump, I discovered that all of my pain did indeed come bearing gifts. Because I had to be creative in finding clothing styles that would suit my small frame, I learned all about fashion, style, and color. From the time I was thirteen I was working in women's retail stores selling clothes and helping women create styles that brought out the best in their bodies. I was great at what I did because I was sensitive to how painful it is to have a body that doesn't live up to one's wishes.

The unfolding of all my emotional traumas allowed me to develop a new relationship with my body. Instead of resenting it for being thin and weak, I was able to embrace the grace and agility of my long, lean bones. This ingredient in my recipe has continued to serve me throughout my adult life. It served me when I worked as a media trainer and as an image consultant. Even today in my coaching programs, where I train people to lead seminars and to be in front of people, one of the gifts I bring is supporting people in returning to their natural style so that their looks don't get in the way of their message.

We create a story around every incident in our lives. These stories set our internal boundaries, which dictate what we can and cannot do. We need to take note that each of these little dramas, each lump in our batter, weaves its way into the bigger stories of our lives. I would never have guessed that my feelings of inadequacy around playing sports were just the tip of an iceberg and that they would lead me to discover and heal a deeper issue about my body. Embracing the pain of my past allowed me to transcend the limitations of my story and gave me access to more joy in my life.

WHERE ARE YOUR LUMPS?

Our emotional wounds prevent us from taking the leap outside our stories, because the pain acts like an invisible fence that traps us inside. We have thousands of different experiences in our lifetimes, but only certain ones remain in our consciousness, replaying themselves over and over again. These are the lumps in our batter that are sometimes visible, other times hidden. Either way, we need to search them out and integrate them.

Take a moment right now and close your eyes. Take a deep breath and ask yourself, "What incident or event from my past is still causing me pain, anger, or regret?" Something will arise, and when it does you will have just uncovered one of the lumps in your batter. It may have happened two days ago or twenty-two years ago. It doesn't matter. If you want to be free to use your story instead of your story using you, you need to integrate all aspects of your drama.

The lumps in our batter are nothing more than the unprocessed events of our past. Once we uncover and accept what each lump consists of, we can begin to integrate all the ingredients in our recipe. Integration spontaneously occurs when we discover the gifts of our past. Hidden inside the darkness of our most painful times are the lessons we need to learn. Integration requires us to view our lives as teaching tools and to honor all that has happened to us. Once we can see our past and everything in it as our teacher and our guide, we will know that we have deeply integrated all the ingredients in our recipe. We will no longer waste our time wondering why certain things have happened to us, and we will no longer resist our stories. Integration equals freedom. We will finally be able to stop—stop trying to fix, change, or make better the story of us. Instead we will have taken an important step on the journey outside our story.

PROCESSING YOUR LUMPS

When Allie was eight years old and in the second grade, her mother dropped her off at school one day. Before heading off,

Allie's mom gave her a big hug and told her she would be back at two o'clock to pick her up. After school Allie walked to where all the moms and dads drove up to pick up their kids. Allie quickly found a spot for herself and stood there anxiously, ready to go home after her long day at school. Allie watched one car after another drive up, fill up with kids, and drive away. Twenty minutes later all her friends had disappeared and she was left standing all alone. Not knowing what to do, she kept looking around up and down the street for her mother. But her mother never came. By the time the parking lot had emptied completely, Allie was feeling lost and desperately afraid. Certain that her mother had forgotten her, and not knowing what else to do, she began to walk home alone. Feeling embarrassed and ashamed that she had been forgotten, Allie slouched her shoulders and let her head droop low in hopes that no one she knew would recognize her.

That day in the second grade, Allie made some decisions that would affect her the rest of her life. She decided that there must be something wrong with her and that that was why she had been left behind. This became Allie's story. Allie made her mother's absence mean she didn't belong and therefore she wouldn't be loved. After all, she reasoned, if she were okay and if she belonged, her mother never would have forgotten her that day. She also decided then and there that she couldn't depend on people. Sitting with me twenty years after this incident, Allie could still feel the pain tearing at her heart. We had just uncovered an unprocessed lump in Allie's batter, one that was still driving her to this day, limiting the amount of intimacy she experienced in her personal relationships and the level of responsibility she allowed herself to accept at work. Allie desperately wanted to learn the lessons of this painful incident—to find its gifts—and move on with her life.

I asked Allie to make a list of all her current behaviors that resulted from the conclusions she had drawn that day—that she was unimportant and a bad girl. I asked her to write about all the ways those conclusions had negatively affected her life. Allie's list looked liked this:

I always have to go out of my way to be extra nice to people and do whatever I can to make them happy.

I always follow the crowd so I won't be left out.

I compromise my own needs for the needs of others.

I can't speak up and say what I think or feel, because then I might get left behind.

I have to give all my power away to others.

I then asked Allie if she could see that she was still making her mother wrong for forgetting her that day. Although she had a great relationship with her mother, Allie could see that she still held some resentment from that incident. She could also see that she unconsciously made her mother wrong each time she found herself acting out one of the behaviors she'd listed. Allie had done years of therapy and other work on herself, and was stunned to discover that she was still making her mother wrong. I then asked Allie what she was getting out of holding on to this incident. She slowly replied, "I get to be right in my belief that you can't really count on anyone and that people aren't there when you need them."

The next step was for Allie to think about and write down all the times that she co-created similar scenarios in her life. After all, she found some comfort in affirming her story's truth. Allie found that in more than five other relationships, she was able to prove to herself that she was unimportant and that people wouldn't be there for her. It was a familiar story, and she knew it all too well. Allie had replayed this story line countless times in her life—not only in her major relationships but in little ways, like allowing herself to be passed over for a promotion or letting people cut in front of her in line at the drugstore. Each time she was ignored or left behind, Allie not only had the satisfaction of being right about being unimportant, but she also got to make her mother wrong all over again for leaving her that day. Twenty years later, after losing a job and experiencing yet another failed relationship, Allie was ready to integrate this incident with all its pain.

I asked Allie to close her eyes, look inside, and ask herself what she needed to do to heal from the effects of this incident. She said she wanted her mom to write her a letter telling her how sorry she was and acknowledging the pain that her actions had caused. Allie knew that her mother might not want to do this, but she felt she needed to ask anyway. I told her that if her mom was opposed to the idea she could just as easily write a letter to herself from the perspective of her mom. Allie called her mother, and even though her mom could hardly remember this event, she was more than willing to write the letter, knowing that it would support Allie's healing. This is what her mother wrote:

Dearest Allie,

This is a letter of apology to you for the incident you shared with me when we last spoke. How hurt you were as a little girl when I promised to pick you up from school and I didn't show up for you. I'm so sorry that you had to have this experience. I wish I could change the past but I can't. I can't imagine all the fear and abandonment that you must have felt and how scared you must have been. When you shared with me I could hear in your voice all the pain and suffering that you experienced.

I would like to tell you how sorry I am for that experience. You mean the world to me. I never meant to hurt you in any way. I'm glad that you shared this incident with me so that this experience can be healed. I hope this letter can heal some of the hurt and help you to find closure. If I can do anything else to help you in this process, please let me know. I love you and I take total responsibility. Please forgive me.

Love you,
Mom

Allie read these words and wept with a mixture of sadness and joy: the sadness of a little girl lost and alone, and the joy of a grown woman healing from the pain of her past.

After Allie had spent a few days with the letter from her mom, she was ready to take the next step of extracting the wisdom that this trauma held for her. Again, I asked Allie to close her eyes and consider what she had learned as a result of that incident. Allie told me that because of that event she had decided she never wanted people to feel unimportant or left out. So she became an accountable, reliable, and trustworthy friend and family member. Looking at me not with the pout of a hurt child but with the certainty of a grown woman, she said, "If I tell you I'll be there, I'll be there no matter what. Showing up for people is a priority in my life. I am sensitive to people's needs and always try to show them how important they are." I then asked Allie how these gifts have served her in her life. It was easy to see how her warmth and caring had helped so many people and how it drove her to want to help, teach, and care for children. Her commitment to people is one of the things she loves most about herself. Standing in the presence of these gifts, Allie could appreciate the wisdom and the value she had gained from the trauma that had haunted her for so long. I explained to Allie that her feelings of being unimportant and left behind would most likely continue to arise because they had been with her a long time. The question was not how she could get rid of those feelings but how she could be kind and compassionate to herself even while she was feeling them. I reassured Allie that if she could love and accept herself even when she was feeling unimportant or left behind, she would be able to use the pain as part of her recipe. We both agreed that the qualities born from her pain would be vital to her in the future.

THE INTEGRATION PROCESS—STEP BY STEP

There is a distinct process that I used with Allie to help her make the transformation from a victimized little girl to an empowered woman aware of her unique gifts. This process works no matter what the specific details of a person's story may be.

1. *Unconceal the issue or emotional wound that is currently causing you pain.* This could be something that is happening in your present-day reality, like a difficult relationship or an ongoing issue with your body or your finances. Or it could be an event from your past that still has you feeling scarred, wounded, or victimized. Once you have identified the lump in your batter, begin by asking yourself, "How does this make me feel?"

2. *Close your eyes and ask yourself, "When have I felt these same feelings before? What incident from my past does this remind me of?"* Allow a scene from an earlier time in your life to come into your awareness, and view the incident that comes to mind in as much detail as you can.

3. *Ask yourself, "What did I make this event mean about me?"* The meaning we assign to the events of our lives is the source of our emotional pain, not the event itself. Each of us interprets the events and circumstances of our lives differently. The meaning we assign to our life's experiences will determine whether we use the event to empower ourselves and move us forward or to disempower ourselves and keep us stuck.

   Vanessa and Emma are sisters who were both young girls when their father walked out on the family. Vanessa, the younger sister, liked having her mother all to herself and enjoyed the peace and quiet that was present in the house when she didn't have to listen to her parents fight. Emma had an entirely different take on the situation. She made her father's walking out mean that she was unlovable, and she felt ashamed because she didn't have a real family. This incident didn't show up as a lump in Vanessa's batter, but it was a huge lump in Emma's. When you uncover the decision you made about yourself, you may discover that it is a recurring theme in your life story.

4. *List the behaviors and the recurrent patterns that have resulted from this decision.* For example, if you decided that you were unworthy, unlovable, or not good enough, look for other experiences that have validated that decision.

5. *Look at whom you blame for the limiting decision you made about yourself and whom you get to make wrong for all that has happened to you as a result of that decision.* You really want to look for all the ways, all the times, and all the situations in which you've gotten to prove you were right and make the other person wrong. Whom do you get back at every time this theme replays itself and you find yourself engaging in self-defeating patterns?

6. *Close your eyes and ask yourself, "What needs to happen for me to heal this incident?"* Is there a ritual you could perform that would help you process the pain that surrounds the incident? Is there something you need to

say or something you would like someone else to say in order to feel complete? Writing is a great way to process lumps—whether you free-write to express your feelings or actually write a letter to the person involved.

7. *Uncover the gifts this incident has given you.* This is the final—and most important—step in this process. Make a list of everything you have gained, everything you have learned, and everything you now know as a result of having experienced this incident. For example, if for your entire life you were put down by your parents and told you were stupid, you may have made the decision to study hard, excel in school, and make something of your life. But now that you've done these things, instead of basking in the joy of your accomplishments, you are still stuck in resenting your parents. To find the gift of this experience, you need to search out every positive insight and lesson this incident has brought you. You might ask, "What wisdom can I contribute to the world that I couldn't have if that event hadn't happened?" Being called stupid as a child can make you more compassionate toward your own children. It can drive you to study hard, to be better educated and well read. The gifts can show up in many ways, and for each of us the gifts will be different. Recognizing these gifts is a vital step in our healing process, because until we find the blessings in the negative events in our lives, those experiences will continue to have control over us. Transcending our stories requires us to extract the gifts, lessons, and wisdom from

each of the events that have dramatically influenced us. Once we embrace those events, we will be able to blend together all of who we are in a giant mixing bowl and integrate the ingredients into our consciousness. In embracing both the pain and the gifts that these incidents have brought, we see how our lives have been designed and shaped for a unique purpose. Only then will the contribution that is hidden within our personal dramas be revealed.

Here is another story that illustrates how this process works. As you read it, try to distinguish each of the individual steps in the process.

Natalie came to see me after she had been in a relationship with Jeff, a sensitive and loving divorced man, for six years. Although Jeff possessed every attribute she had ever wanted in a man, Natalie spent a good portion of their time together feeling angry and withdrawn. For reasons that were unknown to her, no matter how often Jeff reassured her of his love, Natalie always felt less important to him than his son, Jesse. Natalie told me that she spent a lot of time and effort competing with Jesse for Jeff's attention, and that when she lost—which she often did—she acted out like a sulking child. On several occasions Natalie resorted to locking herself in her room when Jesse came for visits. Even when Jesse wasn't with them Natalie put all of his pictures away because it was too painful for her to acknowledge that Jeff shared his heart with another.

Knowing that her current issue with Jeff and Jesse had to stem from an earlier unhealed emotional wound, I asked Natalie to close her eyes and look back in her life to another time when she felt she was not good enough to get the love she wanted. Natalie told me that when she was eleven or twelve years old her mother had a nervous breakdown and was put in a hospital. While her mother was away, Natalie's father showered her with gifts: clothes, perfume, and—most important—his undivided attention. Even though Natalie missed her mother, for the first time in her life she felt deeply cared for and special and close to her father. When her mother arrived back home a couple of months later it was not the happy and joyous reunion that Natalie had anticipated. Instead, her mother began probing, questioning why she had so many new clothes and perfume and other special treats. Her mother was clearly angry that her father had paid her so much attention while she was away. All of a sudden Natalie was aware of her parents quarreling about her, and at the same time she felt her father pulling away from her, putting an end to the close bond they had shared. The pain of that separation was still present in Natalie to this day. I asked her what she had made her father's detachment mean about herself. She told me she had made it mean she wasn't good enough to be loved and she wasn't important enough to get the attention she needed.

I then asked Natalie to make a list of all the ways this decision had negatively impacted her life. Here is her list:

After I felt my dad withdraw from me I began to dress seductively, trying desperately to draw attention to myself.

I became angry and resentful if the man I was dating paid

attention to any other women, whether it was his mother, his sister, a waitress, or an old friend.

Since the time I was a young woman I've always had the need to control the men in my life. I manage their time and need to know where they are going and who they are going with.

I humiliated myself countless times by acting out in jealousy and rage when I didn't get the attention I wanted.

I was so insecure that I broke off relationships with great men because I didn't feel they were willing to make me the most important person in their lives.

Natalie easily saw how this one incident, and the conclusions that accompanied it, had impacted every relationship she had ever had with a man. I then asked her to close her eyes and try to see whom she got to keep making wrong by acting out these behaviors. In an instant she spurted out, "My mother." Natalie was surprised by this response, because she had always felt that she blamed her father for his detachment. But in this moment Natalie could see that she blamed her mom for her father's detachment, sensing that her mother had forced him to choose between the two of them. Natalie realized that every time she acted out in jealousy and every time she sabotaged another relationship, she got to point her finger at her dead mother and say, "See what you did to me? It's all your fault." Now, letting out tears of sadness, Natalie told me that her mother, in the days preceding her death, had been in a coma. One evening right before she died her mother woke up and looked around. Natalie rushed to her side, held her hand, and said, "I love you, Mom." Natalie's mother then spoke the last words Natalie would ever hear from her: "You do?" Natalie wept as she confessed that those words had haunted her for twenty-five years. I asked Natalie what she had made her mother's words mean about herself. Natalie told me she had decided that her mother's "You do?" meant "Who cares?" But this time in recalling her mother's words she took them to mean "How could you still love me?"

I asked Natalie to look inside and see what it would take to heal this incident, to integrate this lump in her batter that had caused her so much pain. I also encouraged her to spend as much time as possible writing about the incident, to invite other memories and feelings to come to the surface to be healed. When we met a few days later, Natalie told me that one day while journaling she realized that her mother was not a vengeful or hateful person, but a woman scorned and deeply insecure. Her father was a womanizer who had been unfaithful on many occasions. For twenty-five years Natalie had been in therapy, working on her issues with her father, thinking that it was his love she was desperate for. She continued reenacting the same situation from her past, unconsciously trying to get her father's attention through Jeff and other men. By doing the work of integrating this experience, Natalie could now see that it was her mother's love she had been seeking all along. Suddenly Natalie saw her mother's jealousy in a whole new light. Her mother simply wanted love and attention, just like Natalie. This realization brought more tears, but this time they were not the tears of a little girl betrayed by her mom but tears of compassion and true understanding. When I asked Natalie if she had thought of a healing ritual to perform with her mother, she told me that one had occurred to her spontaneously one day as she was going through her old pictures. Natalie's healing ritual was to look at a picture of her mother every night before going to bed and imagine holding her mother in her arms. Then she would say the words that her mother had always longed to hear: "I do love you, Mom. You are important and lovable." By making the commitment to loving and forgiving her mother, Natalie was able to access the part of her that could mother herself.

The last part of the process was for Natalie to uncover the gifts that had been generated by her mother's last words and receive the wisdom that was hidden inside her shadow belief that she is unlovable. The main gift that Natalie shared was that the pain of her own childhood was the primary force in her decision to become a family therapist and that her unresolved issues with her mother and father had given her the insight and compassion she needed to work with her clients. The struggles that Natalie had with Jeff's son have enabled her to be a guide for other blended families, supporting them in creating healthy, fulfilling relationships. And because she knows all too well the pain of not having the unconditional love of her mother, Natalie has become an expert in teaching others how to mother themselves and to meet their own unfulfilled needs.

At first the process of integration might seem overwhelming, because most of us have a lot of unexamined pain from our past. But what I have found from taking thousands of people through this process is that if we are willing to go after the most traumatic incidents first, the secondary traumas and less significant issues will often fall away of their own accord. Often we will find that many of our most traumatic times are linked to one major event that caused us to make a core decision about ourselves, a decision that formed the story of our life. In that moment we birthed one of our core shadow beliefs, which replayed itself through our entire life story.

Since each of us has a unique contribution, unlike anyone else's, we are the only ones who will be able to find our inner treasure. The gift that we are can be seen only when we are ready—when we have embraced all the components of our individual stories; when we have given up our right to make others wrong and blame others for the condition of our lives. Healing the wounds of our past is a sacred process. It's a holy event, a moment when we decide to step out of our dramas, the smallness of our individual selves, and see the sacredness of our existence. By gaining wisdom from our emotional wounds, we break free from our past and are able to grasp something truly amazing—our Divine purpose in this life.

HEALING ACTION STEPS

The following exercise is vital to healing the past and uncovering the gifts that lie hidden within the painful events of your life. It's important that you bring your full attention to the process. Set aside at least a half hour of uninterrupted time, and create an atmosphere that will support you in doing deep inner work. Have your journal and a pen nearby. Remember, all the answers you need are inside of you; you only have to become quiet enough to hear them.

When you are ready, close your eyes and take five slow, deep breaths, using your breathing to relax your body and quiet your mind. Read each question one by one. Then close your eyes and allow a response to emerge from deep inside you. Once you have received the answer to a question, open your eyes and write the answer down in your journal, and then move on to the next question.

What incident from my present or my past is still causing me pain, anger, or regret?

How does this situation make me feel?

When have I had these same feelings before? What incident from my past does this remind me of?

What did I make this event mean about me? What did I decide was true about myself?

How has this decision negatively affected my life?

Whom do I blame for the decision I made and for everything that has happened to me as a result of that decision?

What needs to happen for me to heal this incident? Is there something I need to say or do in order to feel complete?

What have I gained, what have I learned, and what do I now know as a result of having experienced this incident? What wisdom can I now contribute to the world as a result of what I have gone through?

Contemplation

*"Every painful event of my life
has brought me great gifts.
I find these gifts effortlessly."*

MAKING PEACE WITH YOUR STORY

To liberate ourselves from the confines of our stories, we must be willing to give up the comfort of our self-made cocoons. I once heard a story of a young girl who asks a wise old woman, "How does one become a butterfly?" With a twinkle in her eye and a big smile, the old woman replies, "You must want to fly so much that you are willing to give up being a caterpillar." Breaking out of the cocoons of our stories can sometimes be a slow and painful process, but the moment we break away, we liberate our souls and bask in the joy of emotional and spiritual freedom. In order to step outside our stories, we must first learn to love, honor, and cherish them for all the ways they have contributed to us. We must acknowledge the experiences they have brought and the wisdom they have bestowed on us. Then and only then will we be able to make peace with our stories and move beyond them to fulfill our deepest desires.

I'm always baffled by the long-standing grudges we hold against ourselves. Why do we continually blame ourselves for events that happened ten, twenty, thirty years ago? Why do we feel so unworthy of complete and total salvation or of absolution for the crimes of our past? I have spent years dwelling on this question. I have watched people continually sabotage themselves, robbing themselves of all that is truly important and depriving themselves of that which would feed their souls. Is it possible that at some level we are continually trying to kill ourselves—or, if not our entire selves, at least some dark, awful part: the aspects or incidents we feel the most shame about? The destructiveness of self-blame and self-loathing can be seen throughout our society. Addiction, violence, abuse, and underachievement permeate all of our lives.

FORGIVING YOURSELF

I have spent years in the self-help movement, first working on myself and then acting as a guide for others. I have come to understand that the core of healing is self-forgiveness. There is nothing—and I mean nothing—more essential to the healing process. Until we make peace and forgive ourselves for all aspects of our lives and our stories, we will continue to use our past to beat ourselves up and to sabotage our deepest dreams. Self-forgiveness happens when we relax into the vulnerability of our humanity and find compassion for our own internal struggles. When we are able to forgive ourselves we come to understand why we are the way we are, why we believe what we believe, and why we feel the way we feel. My friend Sarano Kelly, the author of *The Game,* says, "When you understand, things will begin to change." As long as we continue to feel bad about our stories, and until we have done everything in our power to understand why they are there, we will continually be drawn back into the confines of our dramas. Only when we accept our stories and forgive ourselves completely will we be able to extract all the wisdom our stories hold. Only then will we be free to live outside the limitations set by our shadow beliefs and our stories.

RESOLVING YOUR UNFINISHED BUSINESS

Until we have come to a place of self-forgiveness, we won't be able to manifest our most extraordinary selves and live the life of our dreams. How can we feel worthy of love, success, abundance, and perfect health when our stories continually remind us that we are flawed, insignificant, and unworthy? How can we wake up in the morning calling forth the best from the Universe when we beat ourselves up about our selfishness and continue to feel bad about leaving our relationships? How can we openly receive Divine grace knowing that in our past we ripped off our brother or sexually assaulted our sister? How can we honor ourselves knowing that we continually ignore the callings of our own inner voice? Our unfinished business is the source of our guilt. Layne and Paul Cutright, in their book *Straight from the Heart,* say, "A guilty mind expects punishment. Guilt will cause you to attract people and/or situations to validate your unresolved guilty thoughts about yourself." Our guilt comes from not listening to ourselves, from making choices that go against our core beliefs, from disappointing those we love, and from choosing behaviors that we might feel are selfish. The source of our guilt is that we think we have done something wrong or bad. We fear and expect that we will attract the punishment we feel we really deserve. To the extent that we haven't cleaned up the unfinished business from our past, we will unconsciously punish ourselves by withholding the love, success, and abundance we desire.

MAKING PEACE WITH YOUR INNER JUDGE

Until we make peace with our internal judge and jury we will never allow ourselves to feel and receive Divine forgiveness. Our inner judge knows the difference between right and wrong. Imagine that lying beneath the surface of our consciousness is a great scale of justice that knows our highest good. I like to think of this inner knowing as a set of karmic scales. Our internal karmic scales know when we have violated ourselves and when we have violated others. It knows when we are out of balance. Our karmic scales represent our inner knowing, our internal sense of integrity—the part of us that knows what is right and what is wrong. This inner judge holds our internal scales of justice, supporting us in honoring the integrity of the human spirit. All of us have had the experience of crossing the lines of our own inner knowing. All of us have at one time or another heard the voice of intuition and decided to shut it out or block it off so that we could stay in our stories and attend to our own agendas. But each time we ignore our intuition, each time we fail to listen to our inner voice, every time we follow our heads and not our hearts, we are actually committing a violation against our deepest selves. Those violations are what keep our karmic scales out of balance, and keep us locked inside our dramas. Until we learn to honor the sacredness of our inner knowing and our intuition, we will create pain and drama to guide us back in the direction of our highest selves. Imagine that within the package called "You" came an operating system to hold you to the highest expression of yourself. This operating system is your guide, letting you know when you are on track and when you are off. Its only job is to support you in manifesting your most extraordinary self. It is your own personal guide; it has no agenda other than fulfilling your personal mission and supporting you in bringing forth your gifts to the world.

How is it that we get disconnected from this guidance system? How do we separate from the Universal stream of intelligence that flows so naturally through us? At some point in our lives all of us have been told that our feelings are not important. We might even have been cautioned that if we continued listening to our inner urges and callings we would be ousted from our families, punished or separated from those we love. These mixed messages confuse us, and gradually we begin doubting ourselves and our own inner knowing. Instead of trusting in our own truth, we unconsciously disconnect from our internal operating system. Slowly we lose touch with our own internal sense of what is right and wrong. No longer connected to our inner light that guides us, we decide to follow our parents or other people who look like they are doing okay in their lives. Eventually we forsake our own inner voice entirely so that we can feel like we fit in and belong.

VIOLATIONS OF SELF

Many of us get alarmed and inspired into action when we witness violations in the world. When someone is mugged, raped, or abused, we feel an immediate sense of injustice. It is more difficult to catch sight of the violations we perpetrate against ourselves, for we often violate ourselves in seemingly small and unnoticeable ways. We violate ourselves when we don't listen to ourselves or trust our instincts or claim what we want. We violate ourselves when we shut down our dreams, when we don't take the time to care for ourselves, or when we don't make our inner lives a priority. We violate ourselves every time we deprive ourselves of appreciation and acknowledgment for our hard-earned efforts and every time we deny our special gifts. We violate ourselves when we choose to focus more on our flaws than on our beauty. We violate ourselves when we don't give ourselves the nutrition we hunger for, when we make bad choices, and when we refuse to forgive ourselves for being in our present circumstances. We violate ourselves when we withhold compassion from ourselves for the mistakes we've made, when we spend more time listening to the negativity of our Shadow Boxes than to the love of our hearts. We violate ourselves when we look for what's wrong instead of what's right. We violate ourselves when we fail to do what brings us joy. We violate ourselves by keeping ourselves small.

Most of the violations we commit against ourselves go completely unnoticed by our conscious awareness. But our psyches are acutely aware the moment we stray from our own internal guidance systems. I once led a seminar in which I asked people to list all the ways they betray themselves in each area of their lives. Here are some of the things they shared:

We violate our bodies by

overeating

eating food we know doesn't agree with us

cheating on our diets

telling ourselves we are going to exercise and not following through

not taking enough time for rest and recreation

abusing ourselves with cigarettes, alcohol, or drugs

criticizing ourselves when we look in the mirror

paying more attention to our flaws than to our beauty

staying so busy that we cannot hear the signals our bodies send us

listening to our self-loathing internal dialogues

We violate ourselves in relationships by

staying in relationship with physically or emotionally abusive people

doing things for or with friends that we don't want to do

having sex when we don't want to

depriving ourselves of intimacy when we want it

breaking agreements and commitments with others

gossiping about others

pretending to like people we don't

not spending time with our loved ones

withholding our feelings from others

stepping over our personal boundaries or compromising our integrity

making other people's needs more important than our own

We violate our financial security by

spending more than we earn

running up credit card debt

bouncing checks

lying about our income

not saving money

being unconscious about our spending

stealing

ignoring our debts

paying our bills late

Most of us try to achieve transformation even as we continue to commit offenses against ourselves. We think that if we attend only one more seminar, read one more book, or just think happy thoughts we won't have to clean up all the ways we are violating ourselves. We can read thousands of self-help books, meditate every day, and sit at a guru's feet, but if we use the wisdom we've gained only to put ourselves down and diminish our worth, we have violated ourselves. Each time we look in the mirror and see only part of who we are—every time we spend more time listening to our Shadow Boxes, our unconscious internal dialogues, rather than acknowledging our greatness—we have committed a violation of self. When will we stop? When will we see we have become the perpetrators and we are the only ones who can stop the internal violence?

SUBTLE VIOLATIONS

As she does most mornings, Wendy woke up with a resolution to eat well. She specifically made the internal commitment to stay away from bread and sugar—two foods that she knew didn't agree with her. She stuck to her resolution all through the morning, and even at lunch. But in the afternoon, when her co-workers brought in cupcakes from the local bakery to celebrate someone's birthday, Wendy, reasoning that it would be impolite to decline, ate one of the cupcakes. Instantly she recognized that familiar sinking sensation in her gut that was too painful to be with. Filled with resignation, she tossed her commitment to herself out the window and pretended that what she had done didn't matter. She went home that day feeling heavy, lifeless, and disconnected from herself. That night while meditating, Wendy realized that cheating on her diet was a way she consistently violated herself.

Emily, a stay-at-home mother of two, tucked her children into bed after a long and stressful day. "We'll have fun together tomorrow, I promise," she whispered as she kissed them both good night. As she walked out of their room she thought of ways to make the next day special for the three of them. She promised herself she wouldn't watch her soap opera unless her children decided to take naps, and committed to giving them her undivided attention. But by two o'clock the next day, when Zachary and Alice still hadn't shown any signs of wanting to take naps, Emily found herself growing impatient and resentful. Her commitment to enjoying a peaceful day with her children was quickly forgotten, and Emily found herself watching her soap opera in her bedroom while her children cried at her feet. From that point on, Emily's hopes for the day were gone and all three of them were grumpy.

That evening, disturbed by the outcome of the day, Emily went inside herself and asked, "How can tomorrow be a better day for me and my kids?" At that point she got in touch with the resentment that had been building inside her for weeks. Emily needed more time to herself. Emily's own inner child was screaming for "mommy time." She realized that caring for two children all day long while taking no time for her own needs was in itself a violation against herself. And when she was not acting with integrity toward herself she tended to take her frustrations out on her children. Emily saw that in order to bring balance to herself and her family she would need to carve out some time of her own. She came up with the creative idea of trading baby-sitting duties with another stay-at-home mom in her neighborhood. Once she had the time she needed, Emily was able to stay present with her children and follow through on her promises to them. By living inside her own integrity and honoring her deepest truth, Emily was able to make a new choice, one that led her outside the confines of her story.

Our violations against ourselves often camouflage themselves in subtle ways. Even now you might be trying to figure out ways to minimize this conversation. Check in and see. Are you denying this truth? Are you justifying or affirming that this is not you? Look. Look deeply, over the course of the next several days, and identify where you are committing violations against yourself. Are you willing to examine the depth of abuse that you create on a daily basis? Do you continually violate yourself in the name of your story? It's your life; only you have the ability to change it. This is your chance to dig deep. You can look back and see that you stayed in the cocoon of your story, skimming the surface of your pain, or you can look back and see that you challenged yourself, told the truth, took responsibility, and took action that was consistent with the kind of person you desire to be.

BALANCING THE KARMIC SCALES

Making amends for our self-violations is the highest act of honor we can possibly bestow upon ourselves and others. Making amends restores our integrity and is a vital step in making peace with our stories. It is important that we go back through our lives with the intention of making our wrongs right—balancing our karmic scales. This means making amends to everyone in our lives whom we have in some way wounded, lied to, cheated, or betrayed.

I knew that in order to heal and make peace with my life I would have to clean up all the chaos I had caused in myself, in my relationships, and in the Universe. I wanted so desperately to be able to stand in front of the mirror and in front of other people and feel good, not only about my present but also about my past. Over the years I had left many people angry, disappointed, and hurt. I had also committed my share of crimes against nature, institutions, and other people. I had my first shot at cleaning up my past in a twelve-step program, where I learned that I needed to make amends to those whom I had hurt. At first the thought seemed overwhelming. How could I ever do this? The mere idea of walking up to someone and telling them that I had lied or stolen from them made me tremble in shame. It was odd: I thought I had never cared what others thought about me because I seldom experienced any regret, but, standing in front of this project called cleaning up my past, I was sick with fear and shame. My list of victims seemed too long to face, but, knowing that I could never really feel good about myself until I made my wrongs right, I summoned the courage to come clean with those I had hurt and atone for the crimes of my past. I found it hardest to confront past employers and friends of my family, but, person by person, I was able to say I was sorry, pay back money I owed, and take responsibility for who I had been in the past. Little by little my self-esteem started to rebuild itself and I began the miraculous process of feeling good inside. This process enabled me to make peace with my story. Each amend that I made loosened the chains that had tied me to the drama of my past.

If we don't live a life grounded in integrity, we will try to build our transformation on top of a lie. In order to live the life of our dreams, we need to have a strong foundation on which to build who we are and what we stand for. Anytime we are living outside our personal integrity, we put up a wall between ourselves and others, and between ourselves and the life of our dreams. In any area in our lives where we cease to act out of integrity or violate our internal rules, we are cutting ourselves off from the totality of our power and our ability to create what we want. Cheryl Richardson, author of *Life Makeovers,* says, "We all have different sets of internal rules which make up our personal integrity. Most people are unaware of how much energy it takes to live outside of our internal rules. When we restore our integrity we release enormous amounts of energy that can serve our present-day lives."

Our unhealed integrity issues are at the root of our self-abuse. To the extent that we feel out of balance in our inner world, we will deprive ourselves of fulfilling our desires in the outer world. Our self-loathing will call forth from the Universe people and events that reflect back to us our deepest feelings about ourselves.

Remember, *your outer world is a reflection of your inner world*. And the reverse is also true: When we are in alignment within ourselves, we feel worthy of receiving everything we desire. We call forth people and events that are consistent with the fulfillment of our deepest desires, because again, when we are in balance and feel good about ourselves inside, the whole world will reflect our good feelings back to us. To the degree that we do not clean up the integrity issues inside our stories, we will continue to feed the noisy internal dialogue of our Shadow Boxes. Until we have integrity we will never feel deserving or worthy of living our highest life.

KARMIC RESOLUTION

Karmic resolution is the process of restoring our integrity. We achieve it when we make our wrongs right. Karmic resolution opens the way to transcending our stories and gives us access to the self-love we deserve.

Karmic resolution is the process of healing our relationships with ourselves, others, and the world. We want to be careful not to approach this task by asking, "What's the minimum I can do to get off the hook?" or "What will restore my reputation in the eyes of those involved?" Instead, we want to look for the action that restores our own integrity within ourselves. We need to ask, "What can I do to balance my karmic scales?" And we need to be willing to hear the answer that comes from deep inside. I promise you that if you take on the project of restoring your integrity, you will receive more love, peace, and inner freedom than you could ever imagine. When our karmic scales are in balance we naturally open up to whole new levels of self-esteem and worthiness. It is only then that we will feel deserving enough to manifest our deepest desires and bask in the abundance of the Universe.

As long as we are plagued with feelings of guilt and regret, we will be blinded to our magnificence. Jordan, a thirty-five-year-old real-estate developer, grew up on the streets and learned early on how to survive by his wits. Although he became wealthy beyond his wildest dreams, Jordan was still haunted by the violations he committed in his youth and had tried unsuccessfully for fifteen years to make peace with his past. He attended seminars and men's groups, and tried to attain forgiveness by being overly generous with his friends and family. Jordan knew all the right things to say and the right mantras to chant to temporarily absolve himself of guilt, but still, in the quietness of the night, he was left feeling bad about himself. Jordan was a smart, educated, and well-read man, and it baffled him to no end that he couldn't get over his past. The message that overshadowed his accomplishments was "I don't deserve to have it all." Even though he was keenly aware of the theme of his story and the limitations that it held, he struggled to live outside the boundaries of his personal drama. I suggested to Jordan that we look together to see what he had done in the past that he was still feeling bad about. I explained to him that although our minds can forget our misdeeds, our hearts always remember.

Even though he wanted to be free of his guilt, Jordan still resisted the idea that his past wrongdoings could somehow be affecting the present moment. He felt like he was now a good person, even though he admitted to being arrogant and neglectful in his past. I explained that until we make our wrongs right we will continually beat ourselves up and draw forth experiences that mirror back the bad feelings we harbor inside. Our inner knowing demands that we bring back into balance that which we have violated. I told Jordan that unless he could look each and every person he had wronged in the eye, somewhere inside himself he would feel that he was not a good person and would therefore never really feel deserving of total love and forgiveness and never be free to walk out of his personal drama.

Jordan courageously agreed to explore his past with the intention of cleaning up all that was left unfinished. I asked him to close his eyes and look inside for an incident that was still unhealed. He recalled a time when he was eighteen and working as a waiter in a trendy restaurant in San Francisco. He worked at that restaurant on and off for five or six years—taking time off when he needed to focus more attention on his education and coming back when he needed the money. The owner of the restaurant, an older man named Ted, was always gracious to Jordan, allowing him to come and go as he pleased. Jordan confessed that he and others who worked at the restaurant had devised a way to steal money by not entering customers' checks into the cash register. At times Jordan and his co-workers would also help themselves to food and beverages that belonged to the restaurant. Jordan, who was living hand-to-mouth at the time, rationalized his actions, telling himself that because Ted was a wealthy dentist who lived at the top of the hill and owned two other restaurants, he would never miss the money. He also used the justification that everyone else who worked there was doing the same thing. But now, looking at this incident,

Jordan could see that he did really feel awful about treating somebody who had been so gracious and open with him so poorly.

When I asked Jordan what he needed to do to make amends within himself for what he had done, he said that the owner of the restaurant was probably dead by now and he didn't know what to do to make it right. But when Jordan called an ex-manager of the restaurant, he found out that Ted was still alive and still living in the Bay Area. Jordan summoned his courage, picked up the phone, and called Ted. Now in his early eighties, Ted was excited to hear from Jordan. He had always had a fondness for Jordan and had a special place for him in his heart. After a few minutes of small talk, Jordan told Ted that during the years he worked at the restaurant he had stolen roughly three thousand dollars from him and that he was calling to make amends. In what was one of the most deeply moving moments in his life Jordan, with tears in his eyes and an open heart, told Ted that he wanted to send him a check that day to repay him.

Ted broke down in tears after hearing Jordan's confession. Jordan was surprised to discover that Ted's restaurants had gone bankrupt and that he had lost all his money and his big house. Ted went on to tell Jordan how hard he had been struggling, and how he had just tried to get a loan to pay his bills but had been turned down because of his bankruptcy. He told Jordan that while the three thousand dollars didn't mean that much to him fifteen years ago, it was just the sum he now needed to save his condo from being repossessed. As Jordan wrote the check, he felt it was the best money he had ever spent. He felt clean inside and tremendously grateful that he could now give back to somebody he had taken from. He no longer had to cover up the crimes of his past. For the first time he felt like he could look in the mirror and feel good about what he saw. He knew that his internal scales were in balance, and he had a new sense of self-worth and self-respect.

Cori, a participant in one of my coaching programs, has struggled financially for as long as she can remember, and shared with the group that she had no idea why she was unable to make or keep money in her life. The central theme of Cori's story was that she had to be careful, that otherwise people would take advantage of her. Knowing there must be some karmic imbalance keeping her from attaining her goals, I asked her to make a list of all the places in her life where she was out of integrity financially, and to search her consciousness for any incidents from her past that might be preventing her from receiving the abundance she desires.

The first thing on Cori's out-of-integrity list was an incident that had occurred when she was twelve years old. Cori and her girlfriend had gone to a department store and stolen a lot of the kind of merchandise that appeals to young girls—bathing suits, purses, makeup, and accessories. Then they went back to the girl-friend's house, put all the merchandise on the bed, and started adding up their loot. Although at the time she felt excited because she got away with it, some fourteen years later this incident showed up as a huge source of shame.

Committed to restoring her integrity and learning to love herself at the deepest level, Cori knew that she would have to make amends for the mistakes of her past. The first task on her list was to call the Macy's store where she had shoplifted and admit what she had done. After speaking to several different people she was finally transferred to the general manager. When the manager got on the phone, the first thing he said to Cori was "Are you in a twelve-step program?" Cori said, "No, actually I'm in a coaching program and my assignment this week is to clean up my past and restore any issues that are out of integrity within me." Cori proceeded to tell her story to the manager, and at the end she asked him, "What can I do to make amends for my actions?" He was silent for a moment and then said, "Young lady, I'm very impressed with you. In twenty-four years in this business, no one has ever called me with an admission like this. I think the best thing you can do is to donate money to your favorite charity. Thank you so much for calling." Then he added, "By the way, you really made my day." Cori hung up the phone feeling light, elated, and empowered. She felt free of the chains of her past, as though an internal weight had been lifted from her. She no longer had to suppress this incident. Her internal scales were now coming into balance, and she had transformed this bit of darkness into a bright light.

Feeling empowered and stimulated by her newfound freedom, Cori quickly picked up the phone to tackle the second integrity item on her list. When Cori was eighteen years old, on a mission to raise money for a trip to Europe, she had made a fraudulent claim against an airline, saying that her bags had been stolen when in fact they hadn't. Cori had filled out the necessary forms and weeks later received a check for twenty-five hundred dollars in the mail. Cori now felt concerned about how she was going to heal this integrity issue, because she didn't have the money to repay the debt, but she courageously called the airline anyway. After several phone calls she made her way to a top executive, who greeted her with warmth and caring. Cori told her what she had done and asked the woman what she could do to make amends. In her pleasant and soothing Southern accent, the agent replied, "Well, you could certainly write a letter to Human Relations and tell them what you did." Then she added, "Honey, in God's eyes you're already forgiven."

Cori wrote the letter, but afterward she still felt she had more work to do in order to bring balance to her internal scales. Cori then decided to gather old clothes and luggage from all her friends and donate them to a local women's shelter. In telling me this story, Cori realized that it hadn't been enough to say she was sorry; she had to give back more than she took. She realized that hiding her offenses only made her feel bad about herself and that she punished herself through constant self-hatred and a critical inner dialogue. Cori also saw the correlation between her unhealed integrity issues and the fact that she had difficulty making or keeping money. To top it off, Cori now had new insight into why her only trip to Europe was such a disaster. Cleaning up these incidents from her past allowed Cori to see that she didn't have to watch out for other people, that who she needed to watch out for was herself. Cori realized that if she lived a life true to herself and honored her highest integrity, she would feel deserving enough to make and keep the money she earned.

Once we balance our internal scales and restore our integrity, we will no longer be pulled back into the old feelings and thoughts that have been tied to these events. An inner lightness occurs. Balancing our karmic scales brings us back into alignment with our highest selves. Making amends is a gift that we give ourselves. When we have cleaned up our past and feel good about balancing our internal scales, we can then begin the amazing process of self-forgiveness.

MAKING AMENDS TO YOURSELF

The process of forgiveness calls on us to create new behaviors to heal our relationships with ourselves. We must look inside, because for each of us these behaviors will be different. Now is the time to make a commitment to honor ourselves where we have once violated ourselves. Here are some suggestions for transforming our relationships with ourselves.

Tell the truth to ourselves and others.

Take time for the people we love. Schedule time every day to go for a walk, connect, and share what is truly important to us.

Meditate every day.

Volunteer our time to causes and organizations that inspire us to help: children with learning disabilities, reading programs in schools.

Stop gossiping.

Take care of our physical bodies with nourishing food, adequate rest, exercise, fresh air, and recreation.

Take care of our minds and emotional bodies with time spent alone—journaling, reading, praying.

Honor our boundaries and listen to our inner sense of what feels good and what doesn't.

Make a daily connection with the Divine.

Process our painful emotions when they come up so they can be healed.

Keep our checkbooks in balance and clear up our past debts.

Take time to acknowledge ourselves for all we are, for the joy we bring to others, and for the contributions we've made to the world.

Eat foods that nourish our bodies, and stop eating when our stomachs are full.

Feel gratitude every day for what we have.

Making amends releases us from our past and from our stories. It guarantees us a life outside the limitations of our stories. It blesses us with the greatest gifts of all: self-respect and self-love. When we step through the door of forgiveness and begin to treat ourselves and others with love and compassion, a new reality emerges. Choosing forgiveness means making a promise to ourselves that we won't use our past to beat ourselves up and that we will practice extreme care with ourselves. When we can love ourselves when we're crazy, hateful, jealous, or sad, we are truly free. All we need to begin is the willingness to forgive ourselves completely. Nobody can make us forgive. Only we can do it, and the time is now.

HEALING ACTION STEPS

1. Look back over your life, and make a list of the people you have in some way hurt, violated, betrayed, or mistreated. Allow yourself to see the faces of people from your past—past employers, ex-lovers, people you went to school with—and notice the feelings that arise as you think about each of them. On a piece of paper, write the person's name along with a brief description of the action or nonaction you committed regarding that person that left you feeling bad about yourself. Next, take some slow, deep breaths, close your eyes, and ask yourself, "What could I do to totally balance the scales with this person and restore my own sense of integrity?"

2. Write down all the ways you violate yourself on a daily basis. Include obvious as well as not-so-obvious violations. Do you break commitments to yourself? Do you engage in relationships or behaviors you know are not in your highest interest? Do you stop yourself from speaking out when you feel the impulse? It may help you to think about each key area of your life—physical body, relationships, finances, home, environment—and ask yourself, "How do I violate myself in this area?"

3. Design a plan of action to make amends for the violations you have committed against yourself and others. What actions do you need to take in the outer world that will balance your karmic scales? What do you need to do in order to forgive yourself and return to a state of self-love? Make sure that your plan of action is specific, measurable, and objective. What exactly are you going to do, and by when? It might help you to find a buddy—someone you trust—to check in and share with to support you in this process.

Contemplation

*"Magic happens when I restore
my personal integrity."*

Chapter 8

FINDING YOUR
UNIQUE SPECIALTY

Hidden within our stories is a unique specialty that is unlike that of anybody else. This is the priceless reward for all that we have lived, our return to wholeness. Our specialty is our unique recipe, the sum total of our life's experiences. Each of our traumas, each of our emotional wounds, as well as our joys and talents are here to teach us and guide us to the highest expression of ourselves. As soon as we are able to recognize the usefulness of our stories and extract our specialty out of the dramas we have lived, we will stand in awe of the Universe and its Divine Orchestration. We will see, maybe for the first time, how all the pieces of our lives have worked together to give us a contribution that is unmistakably ours. We will then be able to make sense out of the senseless. We will be able to extract wisdom out of our trauma and pain. We will understand why we were blessed with the specific gifts that only we have. With newfound clarity we will be able to see how each event of our lives was perfectly orchestrated to unfold our highest possibilities. We will see the stories of our lives in a new light. Suddenly our parents, our body issues, our fears, our struggles, our wins and losses, our talents, and our triumphs will make sense. We will stand in the certainty that if we hadn't lived everything we have lived, we would never be able to unveil the wisdom of our Divine gift.

CLAIMING YOUR GIFT

We uncover our specialty when we can look at our lives—all our shadows, our light, our negative conclusions, and all our experiences—and ask ourselves, "Now, why would I have needed that belief or experience? How can this event lead me to discover my unique contribution to the world? What can I now contribute, having gone through what I did? What knowledge and insights do I now possess that I never would have developed if I hadn't had that experience?" We'll know that we've truly integrated our stories when we can see and use the gifts they have brought us. When we've extracted our recipe from the drama of our stories, we will be in the presence of our unique contribution. We will be in a position to share our wisdom with the world, and we will be guided to the best vehicle for that expression. When we extract our specialty we allow the world to benefit from the book of our lives. This requires us to look at our lives through a particular lens and ask ourselves, "If my life so far has been training me to do or be something in particular in the world, what would it be?"

Most of us are unable to see the specialty that our story has provided for us. Until we make peace with our past and give up blaming others for the condition of our lives, we will remain blind to our unique gifts. But as soon as we embrace both the light and the dark parts of ourselves and take responsibility for all of who we are, we will open up to the gifts that are ours to share. I always ask people who are stuck in their stories, "If you were to write a book, what would its title be?" Here are a few of the award-winning titles our stories have qualified us to write.

How to Use Your Life to Suffer

How to Torment Yourself in 28 Days

How to Experience Your Negative Inner Dialogue to the Fullest

How to Manifest Not Good Enough in Every Area of Your Life

How to Prove to Yourself and Others That You Are Unlovable

How to Push People Away So You'll Know You're an Unwanted Reject

While any of these books might qualify as a good read, I think most of us would prefer a title that expresses our highest selves. Every experience in our lives has provided us with specific knowledge and wisdom. Everything that has happened to us was Divinely designed to support us in making our unique contribution to the world.

WHAT IS YOUR STORY'S CONTRIBUTION?

Now is the time to look at your story in a completely new way and discover the contribution that it holds. Here are a couple of examples: If your mother left you early in your life and your two ex-wives walked out on you, your specialty could be "When Women Leave: How to Stay Empowered on Your Own." If your drama is filled with needing men to take care of you because you have the shadow belief that you can't take care of yourself, your specialty might be "Teaching Women to Thrive on Their Own." If you were abused by your uncle or date-raped in college, your specialty might be "Teaching Teenagers Self-Protection and Good Boundaries." If you have battled with addiction your entire life and failed, you might be able to share this specialty: "Showing Kids the Depths and Trauma of Addiction."

In order to discover your specialty, you must be committed to using *everything* you have been through to contribute to someone else's life. You don't need to be a college professor or an author to contribute your specialty to the world. You teach by example what you are here to contribute. You may pass it on to your children or share it with your best friend on a hike. You might impart your wisdom at the watercooler at work or at your nephew's twelfth birthday party. Each of us is given opportunities to contribute all the time. It could be at a relative's funeral or when an old high school friend contacts us on the Internet. We don't need to know when or where we will have an opportunity to deliver our gift to the world; we just need to embrace that we indeed have a gift. Standing in the presence of the special gift that we hold, we will experience a deep peace with our stories and be ready for the giant leap out of our personal dramas and into our Divine expression.

OUTGROWING YOUR STORY

At some point in my life it became clear to me that my story was getting me nowhere. I was faced with a choice: I could stay inside it, continue doing what I had been doing, hoping things would get better and striving to find a little more joy or happiness; or I could give up all the safety and comfort of the known and embark on an adventure beyond my story. Down deep in my soul I knew I had a higher calling. I ached for the spontaneity of the unknown. I had grown sick and tired of the predictability of my own life. I felt as though I was all used up inside my story. My drama no longer offered me any surprises or joy. I always knew what would go right, what would go wrong, what goals I could attain, and what I would keep just slightly out of my reach. Finally the day came when I bottomed out and was no longer willing to live inside my self-created limitations. That day I began to pray for the courage to no longer know myself, because the self I knew left me feeling discontented and empty inside. I prayed for the unveiling of my highest self. It wasn't that I minded the self that I had known, but it was a boring saga, and living out each day was like watching a movie I had seen one too many times. In a way I was blessed by having so much inner turmoil, because it accelerated my desire to transcend my story.

While I was going through my divorce it became clear that it was time to transcend yet another of my stories, that it was once again time to sink or swim. I had just given birth to my first child and had unknowingly stepped right into the motherhood drama, complete with all its joys, triumphs, worries, and fears. Wow, was this a story! I worried about how I could live, how I could survive on my own, and how I could afford to create a life for myself and my son.

One day, while I was feeling absolutely suffocated by the limitations of my past, my sister asked me a very powerful question: "What would you need to do to be blissfully happy, contribute to the world, take care of your son, and create the life of your dreams?" As I contemplated that question, I saw clearly that it was time for me to stop being a student and step into the role of being a teacher. It was time to share the wisdom I had spent years collecting. The one talent I really knew I had was that I could find the gift or the blessing in any negative experience. My pain had taught me to become a master at reinterpreting my life's experiences and using them to transform my current reality. The pain and trauma of my past had given me a unique specialty: to bring light to darkness and find the blessings in all life's events. As I assessed my skills and my capabilities I saw that my most valuable possession came from an unlikely source: the pain and struggles of my own past.

Standing at this crossroads, I saw that I could either use the experiences of my life to contribute to others or allow my past and all its limitations to continue to use me. I had to decide which road to take, and that decision had to be backed up with action. I knew that my purpose was to bring light to darkness, to bring healing where there once was pain. When I meditated on how to fulfill this purpose, the message I got was clear: I needed to write. I made the commitment to write every day.

The process of writing every day, whether I felt like it or not, supported me in living outside my story. Although my commitment was strong, I knew I would need a support structure if I were to continue to live the highest expression of myself. I had to take a stand and make a loud declaration: "This is who I am." I told everyone I met that I was writing about embracing the shadow. Not only did I tell friends and family; I went public, sharing my new self with publishers, agents, and spiritual teachers. I had to put myself on the line so there would be immediate consequences if I slipped back into my story. During this period of unveiling my highest self I attracted a whole new group of friends and associates, who had never heard my "poor me" drama. They knew only the story of who I wanted to be. As I made this shift within myself, I found that the world responded to me differently.

Writing a book was something I had always wanted to do, but it had always lived well outside the boundaries of my story. But this was clearly my next step. It was clear to me that I had only two choices. I could continue traveling down my repetitive road to nowhere, collecting more war stories, more scars, and more resignation, or I could make a new choice, go down a different path, and arrive at a place I had never been before. I knew that to accomplish my goal I would need to stay present with my discomfort and my fear of the unknown rather than retreat to the false safety of familiar ground. I made the conscious choice to stop listening to my Shadow Box, which screamed, "You never finish what you start. You're not smart enough to write a book, and nobody will listen to what you have to say, anyway." Instead, I made choices that were outside the realm of anything I had done before. One day at a time, I took actions that were consistent with the person I desired to be rather than the person I had been.

After a few months of consciously choosing to live outside my story, I could tell immediately when I had slipped back in. I could feel that familiar state of resignation coming over me like a dark cloud, carrying with it all the old feelings of self-doubt, uncertainty, and fear. I knew I had stepped back into the limitations of my drama when I again started listening to that small, scared part of me that begged me to stop striving for anything other than the life I knew. It pleaded with me to play small and stay safe. When I had stepped back inside my story I felt insignificant, bored, and lazy. Taking the leap outside my story required me to stop, close my eyes, and acknowledge to myself, "Oh, here I am, back inside my story." Now, standing outside my story, I felt strong and bold, boundless and indestructible. But stepping out of my past and leaving the story I knew so well felt like taking a giant leap off a high cliff. It appeared that the distance I could fall would be deadly. Inside my old story I already felt like a failure, so if I tried something and it didn't work out, no one would notice. But now I had raised the stakes considerably. I had given up my alibis. If I failed at delivering a book, if I didn't show up as who I said I wanted to be, I would be left in the hopelessness and resignation of a life unfulfilled. This thought was so unbearable that it drove me to keep stepping out, taking risks, and moving forward with an intense focus I had never known before. What I found was that the more I wrote about my life experiences in order to contribute to others, the more distance I had from my story. Living true to my purpose gave me access to staying outside my story.

Ultimately, contributing our unique gift and using our specialty will be our salvation. Because when we're using all that we know, all that we have been, and all that we are, we're aligned with the vastness of the Universe and the highest expression of our souls. Our attention and energy will no longer be on us and our drama. This was certainly true for my friend Karen. Karen grew up in a household where she felt verbally abused and unloved by her parents. She cannot remember a time when she didn't hear a voice in her head that told her she was inadequate and defective. By the time she was attending elementary school, Karen had begun using food to mask her pain, suppress her feelings of inadequacy, and provide her with the security she never felt at home. By the age of ten Karen was noticeably overweight, and she remained that way for most of her adult life. Being overweight, of course, further added to her feelings of inadequacy. Feeling fat, undeserving, and stupid, Karen settled for being invisible and rarely spoke up for herself. Instead, she continued to abuse herself with food, stuffing herself in an attempt to silence the harsh thoughts and painful feelings that were always screaming to get her attention. To some extent her strategy worked. Karen felt emotionally numb and disconnected from any sense of passion in her life. The message of her story, which she played out over and over again, was that she was fat and worthless, and that her existence didn't matter.

Then one day after her oldest daughter's wedding, Karen and her family excitedly gathered together to watch the wedding video. When Karen watched herself on video for the first time, she was horrified by what she saw. The feelings of inadequacy she had tried so hard to suppress now rushed relentlessly to the surface. She actually saw the reflection of her shadow story in living color all over the television screen. As years of unprocessed pain washed over her, Karen closed her eyes and held herself close, remembering all the incidents from her past that had left her feeling inadequate, defective, and unlovable. Later, when we spoke, I encouraged her to journal on a daily basis, as a way of healing and releasing the burden of pain she had been carrying for so long. Along with her daily practice of journaling, Karen began meditating, praying, and getting quiet enough to listen to what was going on inside of her.

Several weeks later, when Karen watched the videotape again, she was amazed by what she saw. This time, her excess weight showed up for her not as a source of shame and guilt but as a suit of armor that protected her from the world and cushioned her from her own self-loathing. Having embraced the gift of protection that this armor had offered her for years, Karen was now willing to unzip it and venture outside the safety of her self-deprecating story. Holding on to her excess weight allowed Karen to conceal the truth about herself: that she is worthy of all the love the world has to give. Her physical imperfections and her weight had been her battleground for so long, and now she was committed to leaving the familiar path of self-abuse and stepping into the world of the unknown.

Karen's life changed dramatically after she identified her life's story. Once an aesthetician, she now works as a life coach and helps other women stop numbing and abusing themselves with food. She teaches them to heal the emotions that underlie their weight issues. She coaches them to come out of hiding and to find the courage to express their authentic beauty. She passes on to other women the gifts she gave herself: self-acceptance, security, and the confidence to be seen. When feelings of unworthiness surface in her, as they do from time to time, Karen blesses and embraces them. Most of all she blesses her fat, for it was the driving force behind her discovery of her unique contribution and her decision to share her specialty with the world. Standing outside her story, Karen honors her body as a temple and makes choices that support its well-being.

～ ⌒ ⌒ ～

Taking the step outside our stories is like having a foot in two worlds. As we look down the path of our stories, we know with certainty where it will take us. Even though we may not like the destination, at least we feel confident and comfortable in the knowledge of what to expect. But choosing the unfamiliar road and a life outside our stories calls on us to trust that the Universe will show us the way and give us what we need.

When I met Lyndi a few years ago she was in her early thirties and working as an insurance broker. Her mother and father, both alcoholics, divorced when Lyndi was very young and were rarely around to take care of her or her younger brother. As a result Lyndi was left to fend for herself. Although Lyndi started working at the age of fourteen, she barely made enough money to cover the cost of clothes and school supplies. The story that developed out of Lyndi's childhood is that life is a struggle and that no one is ever there for her so she has to take care of herself. On the outside Lyndi appeared confident and competent, projecting the image that she had it all together. But Lyndi had a big secret: At night, after a day of selling insurance in her office, Lyndi would get in her car and head downtown, where she worked as a dancer at a topless bar as a way of satisfying her seemingly endless hunger for money. Lyndi desperately wanted to lead a more spiritual life, yet she had grown used to the money she earned as a dancer and didn't know how she could make it financially without it. Eventually the fact that she was exploiting her body for money took too big a toll on her self-esteem, and one day she simply couldn't do it anymore.

Committed to stepping outside the life she knew, Lyndi decided to take the money she had saved from her dancing and use it to travel to India. She was really hoping that something huge and dramatic would happen while she was there that would launch her out of her story and into her spiritual essence. But instead she had two subtle but profound experiences that would ultimately change her destiny and give her the courage to step outside her story.

While attending a spiritual seminar in Goa, Lyndi came across a man who was selling the most exquisite pictures of India. She wanted desperately to have those beautiful souvenirs to take home to show her friends and family and to remind her of her spiritual pilgrimage. But when she found out the price of the photographs she knew she could not afford them. A little voice told her to wait until the end of the seminar, that the man would probably sell the leftover pictures at a discounted price, but Lyndi didn't trust this inner knowing and feared that if she didn't act right away there wouldn't be any left for her. So she dug deep into her pocket, bought the photos, and took them back to her room. On the last day of the seminar, as all the vendors were packing to leave, Lyndi noticed that she had been right: There the man was, selling the same photos she had purchased, for a third of the price she had paid. She felt a familiar pang of regret as she walked away.

Lyndi had also set off on her trip with the hope of replacing a bedspread her father had owned. She spent days going in and out of little boutiques, hoping to find just what she was looking for. As her trip came to an end she figured that what she was looking for simply didn't exist, so against her better judgment she bought the closest thing she could find. Then, at the airport in Delhi, while waiting for her plane, she walked into a little store and saw hanging in the back corner the very bedspread she had longed to buy for her father. Unfortunately, by this time Lyndi's bags were full and her pockets were empty. Lyndi was astonished and amazed to realize that, had she trusted the Universe and her inner knowing, everything she wanted would have been delivered effortlessly to her.

Instead of being able to bask in the joy of the Divinity of the Universe, Lyndi came face-to-face with the stifling limitations of her story, which told her she couldn't trust the Universe to take care of her needs. As she told me this story, a deeper truth emerged: Lyndi uncovered her core shadow belief, which said, "I can't trust anyone to take care of my needs." When push came to shove Lyndi always crossed the line of her inner integrity and tried to make something happen, sure that she would never get her needs met in any other way. Lyndi had countless examples showing her that if she would just let go, get out of the way, and give up her story, the Universe would give her exactly what she needed. It became apparent that Lyndi's story and all its drama had given her specific wisdom and a very distinct gift: Lyndi's specialty is to teach others to trust in the Universe, surrender their wills, and listen to their inner knowing. Now a meditation instructor and yoga teacher, she often tells her students, "Listen to your heart and take that leap of faith." Living outside her story, Lyndi has a new mantra: "The Universe gives me everything I need." Lyndi feels blessed to know that God speaks to her through her own inner knowing.

EXTRACTING YOUR SPECIALTY: THE PROCESS

In order to find your specialty you must identify and integrate the significant incidents—both positive and negative—that have led you to become the person you are today. This process requires that you do several things:

1. *Make a list of the significant experiences of your life, including your traumas, victories, loves, losses, successes, and humiliations.* These are the particular ingredients of your recipe, which, once integrated, will give you everything you need to find your specialty and make your unique contribution.

2. *Look for the common theme or themes that each of these events shares.* It might be that loss is the theme that permeates your life story. Or you might discover that your theme is that you have been left out of your family, rejected by your peers, or passed over at work. The

theme that your past reveals might be that you are never good enough—to get the part in the play, to get into the right school, or to find a loyal mate.

3. *Ask yourself, "If I were going to teach a college class based on the incidents of my past, what would the name of my course be?"* You want to look for what your life's experiences have made you uniquely qualified to teach or contribute. What do you know and understand about life that most people don't? What have you learned from all your life's experiences that could benefit someone else?

My sister Arielle is a great example of someone who is using her story and all its contents to empower herself and contribute to the world. Arielle has mastered the art and skill of making things happen. I asked her to share with me some of the significant events and incidents from her past that helped her find and develop her unique specialty. As she looked inside, three events stood out most in her mind. The first occurred one day when she was four years old and attending temple with our family. As they walked into the temple, Arielle overheard Sy Mann, who was at that time the president of the temple, telling another adult that people were talking too much during services. During the service, on a sudden whim, Arielle stood up and began walking up and down the aisles of the temple in her pretty pink dress and black patent leather shoes, shouting at the top of her lungs, "Sy Mann says to shut up!" Suddenly everybody was staring at Arielle, laughing at the candor of this little four-year-old. Arielle remembers feeling ashamed and horrified and deciding she never wanted to be seen again. She spent the next twenty years of her life trying hard to be invisible and to stay out of the limelight.

The second event occurred when she was seven. Arielle was fascinated by fantasy, fairy tales, and magic. As her little sister, I remember having séances at our house and people at school calling me the witch's sister because Arielle had long black hair down to her waist, always wore black, and was into exploring other realities. There was something very different about Arielle; I knew it, and everyone who met her could see it. One of the experiences she will never forget happened when she was seven years old. Arielle woke up in the middle of the night and saw our Grandfather Lou sitting on the foot of her bed. He said, "I came to say good-bye and to tell you that I'll always be here with you." Then the image of him vanished. At that very moment Arielle heard the phone ring, saw lights going on in the house, and heard our mother cry out in pain. A few minutes later our father came into her room and said, "I came to tell you that your Grandpa Lou died." Arielle replied, "I know, Daddy. He already told me." It was at that moment that Arielle knew there was more to life than one could see.

The third event occurred on her first day of college. When Arielle went to sign up for her major in TV production, she was met by the dean of her school, who quickly let her know that there would be no future for women in broadcasting. He told her that she would be much better off in the school of journalism. As a result of taking the dean's advice, Arielle proceeded to learn the ins and outs of journalism, while at the same time sharpening her writing skills. When Arielle finished school she decided that the job that would best utilize her skills and talents was to be found not in journalism but in public relations.

For the next ten years Arielle successfully promoted events for artists, entertainers, and corporations, but still she was left feeling dissatisfied and discontent. Then one day she awoke to the realization that she needed to include her deep spiritual life in her work. All the work she had been doing had been preparing her to practice her very specific and unique specialty and thus make the contribution that was truly important to her. Today she is one of the most powerful and influential people in the spiritual world. Not only does she promote the top spiritual leaders of our times; she is an agent who helps get important messages out into the world and is the author of the *Hot Chocolate for the Mystical Soul* series.

Looking back over these three significant events of Arielle's life, we see two distinct themes emerge. The first is that it wasn't safe for her to be in the limelight. The subtle message that Arielle received both from the incident at the temple and from being told not to pursue a career in broadcasting was to not speak out but stay in the background. The other theme is her deep connection with the spiritual world. When Arielle looked at what her life's experiences had made her uniquely qualified to contribute, she saw that she had the skills, the know-how, and the power to take important messages out into the world. Instead of feeling discouraged and victimized by the events of her life—which she could easily have done—she decided to use her past, her pain, and her gifts to make a difference in the world.

Each of us has this capability, no matter how tragic, tiresome, or satisfying our past. We want to examine our lives and dig out our contribution and our gifts. We have learned things and lived through things others have never experienced. Our experience is what makes us specialists. And the world is in need of what we have to offer. This was true for Johanna, who spent years of her life steeped in a story about what a horrible person she was. When I met Johanna, she was filled with anguish and shame about the fact that she was born and raised in Germany and was part of a culture that had committed horrible atrocities against millions of Jewish people. Johanna struggled with depression, anger, and fear that ran so deep she could barely tolerate the pain. This story consumed her every thought. I knew that in order for Johanna to heal and to step outside her story, she would need to find the gift that her pain held.

I asked Johanna to tell me what it was like to be born in Germany fifteen years after the war. She told me that the early years of her life were peaceful and happy, set among the rolling hills and quaint culture of her small village. But by the time she was eight or nine, Johanna began hearing the stories her parents and grandparents told about the war. She learned from them what it was like to have bombs falling all around you and to have to spend the night hiding in the basement for safety. She imagined the terror of not knowing if mothers and fathers would ever see their sons again. As her relatives shared their painful memories, she was horrified to hear about the fear, suffering, and starvation that permeated that dark time in Germany's history.

When she was in the eighth grade, Johanna watched a documentary at school about the war. This was the first time she had really seen or understood the impact of the massacre that had occurred in her country. Tears stung her eyes and deep shame washed over her as she realized that she was a citizen of a country that had perpetrated horrible violence against the Jewish people. Suddenly an even worse thought arose within her: "If the people of my own country could massacre 10 million people in cold blood, what does that make me? Could I be capable of the same horrible crimes that were committed by my own people?" In that moment Johanna experienced the deep shame of her heritage and took it upon herself.

I then asked Johanna to take the next step and make a list of the significant events from her past that still weighed heavily on her heart. What were the incidents and events from her past that still caused her embarrassment, anger, or shame? And what did she make those incidents mean about herself? Here is the list she made:

I was told as a child that the people of Germany didn't think for themselves but just followed Hitler at the expense of millions of lives. I decided I would never be a part of any organization, fearing that I would lose my ability to think for myself.

Many times during my life people told me, "You're so nice. You're nothing like those Nazis." I decided that if I were outspoken and powerful I might be thought of as an angry German, so I squashed my power and leadership skills and tried to always be nice and demure.

After moving to the United States and experiencing firsthand the animosity that some Americans feel toward Germans, I distanced myself from my German friends and went twelve years without speaking to any of them.

When I visited France, my traveling companion warned me, "The French hate Germans, so tell them you're Swiss or Austrian." I decided that it wasn't okay to be me and began taking on different personas in an attempt to fit in.

When I was young, my mother told me that she used to play with some Jewish kids who lived down the street from her. She said that when the war broke out, one day they just disappeared. I was horrified. The knowledge of this incident made me feel uncomfortable around Jewish people.

When I first moved to the United States, I went to a party thrown by my employer, who happened to be Jewish. As a party game they put the name of a famous person on the back of everyone who walked in. Then each guest had to question the others in order to figure out whose name was on their back. Being overly conscious of my heritage, I prayed that they hadn't put the name of a Nazi on my back. But to my horror the name they'd given me was Adolf Hitler.

When I was young I walked into a café in our small town in Germany. A friend of my grandfather's was sitting at a table, boasting about his loyalty to the Nazi party, saying, "I still wear my brown shirt!" I felt sick with shame and humiliation, and horrified that I was one of them.

After seeing a documentary about the war, I tried to stamp

out anything within myself that could possibly be seen as dark or evil. I strove to never do anything bad to anyone, hoping that this would guarantee that nothing bad would happen to me. I became rigid and controlling, and as a result I rarely experienced any joy.

Having seen the devastation that anger breeds, I never allowed myself to get angry or even maintain healthy boundaries. I thought I had to be nice to everyone, even if they were abusive to me.

It was obvious that the events of Johanna's life had given her a very specific recipe. The next step was for Johanna to find their gifts. I asked her to make a list of everything she now has and knows as a result of her upbringing in Germany. Here is a list of the skills and abilities that Johanna now possesses that she wouldn't have if she hadn't experienced what she did:

Growing up in Germany after the war gave me my love and passion for history. I became an avid reader—trying to learn everything I could about the Holocaust.

I became very interested in self-help and human potential. I turned to psychology in an attempt to understand how a madman could inspire an entire country to commit unthinkable crimes.

Because I hated my heritage, I became good at making new friends and learning about other cultures.

I always had a strong interest in any humane endeavor. I spent the majority of my teenage years protesting against violence and supporting peaceful outcomes.

Because I was horrified by the violence perpetrated against the Jews, I made a commitment early on that my life would be about love, service, and healing.

I developed a strong interest in Judaism and studied the Kabala.

I am driven to look for what people have in common rather than what separates them.

I am good at finding ways to peacefully resolve conflicts, whether between me and my ex-husband or between my kids. Because I don't want anyone to get hurt, I go out of my way to create win-win solutions.

I have learned to be very adaptive and can explain things in many different ways to a divergent group of people.

I learned that as long as I kept quiet about the pain of my past I could never heal my issues and move forward.

I am committed to bringing resolution to the ancestors of the victims as well as the perpetrators of the Holocaust. I am in a unique position to help heal this issue on a global level.

Johanna was able to see the many gifts of the painful experiences she had lived. Yet she still wasn't sure how to use her specialty to contribute to others. Then last year Johanna met Rosemary, who is very active in the Jewish community, and the two became fast friends. One day they began talking about the wounds that still exist between the Germans and the Jews. Johanna shared with Rosemary the pain she has felt about being German, pain she has carried all her life. She told Rosemary that many of her German friends were still living inside the shame of the atrocity that occurred more than forty years ago. Rosemary was touched by Johanna's honesty and shared with her that most of the Jewish people she knew had never even considered how the atrocity had affected the Germans who did not participate in those crimes. After hearing Johanna's point of view, Rosemary could see how this incident had victimized the Germans as well as the Jews.

Johanna and Rosemary then came up with the brilliant idea of making a documentary about the effect the Holocaust had on the generations of both Jews and Germans that followed. Rosemary approached an award-winning documentary filmmaker she had met recently in California, who agreed to produce the film. Everyone who hears about the project is deeply touched and very excited, feeling in their hearts how important this message is in terms of healing the world's pain.

Now that Johanna is working for a higher purpose, she no longer feels shame about her heritage or any of the incidents from her past. For the first time she truly understands the deeper purpose of the pain and inner turmoil she suffered all those years. In fact, she blesses her pain, for it gave her the wisdom she needed to make a difference to the world. Johanna cried as she told me that all her life she had been asking herself, "What am I here for?" and now she knows. Being a part of something greater than herself has given Johanna the peace she always longed for. She takes better care of herself now—from what she eats to how she speaks to herself—because she knows that she is the bearer of a precious gift that is intended to bring healing to the world.

Johanna's work paid off. She has found the specialty that lay hidden within her painful life story. Her new commitment is to be a catalyst for healing between the Germans and the Jews. Johanna shared with me recently that had it not been for her willingness to work through her shame and process the lumps in her batter, she never would have had the courage to even initiate a conversation with a Jewish person.

Our specialties are often birthed out of our pain. They are one of the unique gifts that we have to contribute. There is no right specialty, and no two are the same. Our specialty is what enables us to use our stories instead of having our stories use us. It is our unique way to contribute to the world, to know that we make a difference and that our trials and tribulations have not been in vain. The process of finding our specialty causes us to reinterpret our life's events, to assign new meanings that will lift us up and propel us outside the limitations of our stories. We all have a choice. We can choose to mix the recipe we were given into a purposeful masterpiece that will feed our souls and nourish those around us. Or we can allow our precious recipes to remain uncooked. Unconcealing your unique specialty is the most vital step you can take in transforming your life and living outside your story. Using your specialty will allow you to stand tall and feel empowered and proud about yourself and your life.

HEALING ACTION STEPS

1. Identify ten incidents—both positive and negative—that have significantly affected your life. Reflect on each one, asking yourself,

> What skills and abilities do I possess because of this experience?

> How can I use this incident to contribute to myself and others?

> If my life were training me to fulfill a particular need in the world, what would it be?

2. Imagine that you have been asked to teach a college course based on the culmination of all your life's experiences. What would the name of that course be?

Contemplation

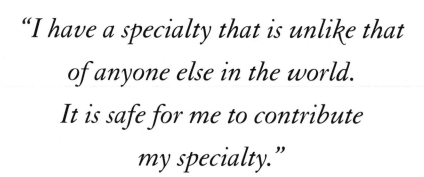

*"I have a specialty that is unlike that
of anyone else in the world.
It is safe for me to contribute
my specialty."*

Chapter 9

LIVING OUTSIDE
YOUR STORY

Living inside our stories guarantees us a life filled with fear and wanting. The fear tells us to watch out, to hide, and to play small so we won't be exposed. The wanting drives us to violate our souls, trying to grasp on to anything that might make us look or feel better. When we are wanting, when we are grasping, when we are judging ourselves or others, we can be sure we are in our stories. Outside our stories, there is no wanting. There is only the belief and the inner knowing that everything is as it should be. By listening to our internal dialogue and checking in with ourselves often, we will be able to distinguish at any moment whether we are inside or outside our stories.

Outside the confines of our personal dramas, our internal dialogue reflects the unlimited possibilities that are available to us at every moment. Outside our stories we are filled with feelings that reflect our highest selves rather than those that echo our lowest thoughts. We are filled with an inner knowing that says, "I trust that the Universe will take me where I'm supposed to go. I love life. Everything is unfolding in Divine order. I have enough. I am enough. I am blessed. I can do it. I believe in myself. Good for me! How can I serve you?" Outside our stories we bask in excitement, joy, abundance, openness, enthusiasm, exhilaration, trust, gratitude, awe, inner knowing, self-confidence, appreciation, respect, unconditional love, and boundless energy.

STEPPING OUT

All of us have days when our internal dialogues are more consistent with our personal dramas than with our greatness. In order to step out of our stories, we first need to be able to recognize that we are in them. We need to be able to say, "This is my story. These are my shadow beliefs. This is my Shadow Box that screams at me all day long." If when we get up in the morning the first thing we hear from our Shadow Box is "You're worthless. You're never going to get what you want" or "You look terrible, why don't you eat better?" most of us, instead of saying, "Oh, I'm in my story. . . ," just step right into it. We go for it. We bite the hook. We get enrolled. Not only do we listen to that voice, we *become* that voice; and instead of watching the movie we become the star of the show.

Recently I spent time with Ethan, a thirty-nine-year-old holistic healer, who shared with me how completely different he feels when he is in his story compared with when he is free from its limitations. "I'm not safe in the world" is the theme of Ethan's story. Intrigued, I wanted to hear more.

Like a lot of people, Ethan has been traveling the path to self-improvement for many years. Committed to transforming himself, he searched high and low, learning technique after technique, trying to feel some inner safety and become more than he'd been. Ethan knew there was more inside of him than he'd been able to tap into. Frustrated by his inability to succeed in his career and in his desperate need to feel safe, Ethan numbed himself with marijuana, hoping to find there the peace and contentment he desired. Committed to breaking down the barriers that stood between the self he knew and the self he dreamed of, Ethan enrolled in my coaching program. One of the first exercises he was assigned was to identify the stories around each aspect of his life. Ethan began by examining his story around why he smokes pot. His story told him that smoking pot enhanced his creativity and increased his self-confidence, but the truth was that pot distanced him from the life he desired. His addiction separated him from both his pain and his passion. I asked Ethan to identify the feelings as well as the other behaviors that live inside this story.

Living inside the confines of his story, Ethan would spend hours each day getting stoned and fantasizing about what his life could be like. He would daydream about different projects and pretend that his endless planning was actually getting him somewhere. Ethan was always "getting ready" to take action, but he never stepped into the arena of making it happen because he was too afraid. Inside his story Ethan was afraid to share his dreams with people, feeling that doing so would take away his momentum and his ability to manifest them. Concerned with being accepted, Ethan feared the disapproval of others, who he felt might not support him in his goals.

Inside his story Ethan felt like he was small and the world was huge. On any given day he would feel fearful, anxious, numb, angry, resigned, hopeless, and victimized. Inside his story Ethan constantly felt unsafe, so he'd hide and try to remain unnoticed.

One morning after another night of fantasy and delusion, Ethan looked at himself in the bathroom mirror and saw a man getting old without having lived his dreams. He saw the face of a great impostor, someone who was still pretending he was on his way to success when in fact his story was going nowhere. After years of working on himself, Ethan made the decision to give up marijuana and to live outside his story.

Now, standing outside his story, Ethan has been able to open his heart and feel safe exposing his feelings to those around him. Today he shares his plans for the future with people before he even knows how to make them happen, confident that he will be guided to the right action. Outside his story, Ethan spends much less time planning and more time taking action. He is less concerned with being accepted and allows himself to try new things whether he knows how to do them or not. Outside his story, Ethan takes care of his health, honors his body, and does not smoke pot. Ethan shared with me that he feels good enough about himself to be influential whether he's liked or not.

When he is unencumbered by the limitations of his personal drama, Ethan feels connected, optimistic, creative, confident, supported, and safe in the world. Outside his story he feels masterful;

life for him is a palette of infinite possibilities to choose from. He feels honest and authentic, powerful and productive. Most of all, he feels like he matters.

ARE YOU IN OR OUT?

One of the most important steps in getting outside our stories is being able to recognize when we are living inside them. Suzanne was a participant at a recent workshop where we had been discussing the limitations of our stories. She shared with me that on the last day of the process she had gotten up early and was sitting on the deck of her hotel room, which overlooked a beautiful bay. She told me the scene could not have been more perfect, and that she felt totally at peace. Sitting on a comfortable couch near the window, she opened the sliding glass door to breathe in the sea air. Suzanne decided this was the perfect setting to take in a few minutes of quiet meditation. She closed her eyes and began to breathe deeply. But within seconds she recalled a humiliating incident that had occurred with a man some twenty years earlier. Suzanne was horrified. Her moment of peace and quiet was rudely interrupted by this memory, and soon she found herself feeling victimized, humiliated, and powerless as she replayed the incident over and over in her mind. In an instant she was thrown right back into the middle of her story, which told her she wasn't good enough to be treated with respect. Instead of stepping back and saying to herself, "Oh, look, I'm back inside my story," she started listening to the same Shadow Box she had listened to thousands of times before. It wasn't long before Suzanne's mood of peace and tranquillity was replaced by anger, oppression, and self-loathing.

Just then a group of ducks walked by the open sliding glass door, seemed to stop directly in front of her room and say, "Quack, quack, quack." Suzanne opened her eyes in disbelief. It was like a message from the Universe telling Suzanne that she had dropped back into her story. It was as though the ducks were mirroring her internal dialogue: "Boo-hoo, poor me. Quack, quack, quack." She couldn't help but laugh, and decided she would use the phrase "quack, quack, quack" to catch herself whenever she slipped out of the fullness of her being and back into her story.

BECOMING THE OBSERVER

In order to transcend our dramas, we must make the commitment not to use our stories to beat ourselves up anymore. We have to be willing to stop indulging our dramas, to stop empowering them with our attention. If you have ever practiced meditation, you have probably noticed that your mind is a constant stream of thoughts. But if you are committed to your meditation practice, you make the choice to simply observe your thoughts instead of following them where they are trying to lead you. With practice, what you find is that at some point your mind realizes that you are not going to bite the hook and it gives up. It lets go, and you're just there witnessing the workings of your mind. The same is true for our stories. If we don't act out our dramas, we can *choose* to walk away from them. The most important thing we can do to break free from our dramas is to acknowledge them as stories rather than crawling inside them, believing them to be the truth. Instead of blindly following the instructions of our Shadow Boxes, we can say, "Oh, thanks for that thought. But right now I am choosing a different thought." Eventually our stories will stop replaying themselves, because they can exist only when we believe we *are* our stories. Our stories feed off the attention we give them.

If there is no dialogue between us and our stories, they will cease to have any control over us. We simply make the choice to dis-identify with them. We do this by declaring out loud, "Oh, here we go again. I'm in my story." It's like watching television. We can choose to walk away, even though the television is still droning on and on. The question we want to ask ourselves is, "Do I want to feed my story and give it my life force? Do I want to empower it with my precious energy?" If our answer is yes, then by all means we should sit down in front of our story and listen to it. But we need to do it consciously. We all have the right to indulge in our story from time to time. We might say to ourselves, "It's Tuesday afternoon at two and I have nothing better to do. I think I'll sit down for a while and replay my personal drama." Then at least we can be responsible for what we are creating.

STRATEGIES FOR GETTING OUTSIDE YOUR STORY

There are infinite choices available to us if we choose to transcend our stories. We could go inside and have a dialogue with our story;

we could "free-write" and allow that part of us to express itself. We could say, "Excuse me. I know you want something here, but I have other things to do today." Or we could choose to talk to God. There is a saying, "When you're thinking about God, you're not thinking about your problems." The vibration of our story and the vibration of our deepest self are totally opposed to one another. We cannot experience both at the same time.

It's important that we identify some strategies to get outside our stories when we find that we have slipped back inside them. Here are a few strategies we can use to dismantle our stories and gain access to the life that awaits us outside the limitations of our personal dramas.

Ask the people who were involved in your emotional traumas to give you their version of the story. Embracing a new perspective lets us know immediately that what we have identified as our story is only one version of the truth. While I was writing this book I e-mailed the first few chapters to my older brother, Mike, a trial consultant, to get his feedback. In his reply he pointed out what I believe is a very important distinction:

> The stories of our lives are 90 percent perception and 10 percent fact. Every person we know will view the same set of facts in a different way. In my job as a jury consultant, I listen to lawyers every day take the same collection of undisputed facts and mold these facts into stories that serve the best interests of their clients. There is little or no search for the truth; there is only a collection of arguments that will be perceived in different ways by different people. Unfortunately, in our personal lives, many of us choose to

view our lives from the perspective that is least favorable to us. By doing that, we become victims with someone to blame for our misfortune, rather than taking responsibility for the portion of our fate that is a result of our own choices.

Later that night Mike called me again. "By the way, Debbie," he said, "I just have to tell you something. That story you wrote about your childhood isn't true." "What do you mean it isn't true?" I asked. "I lived it!" "No, Debbie," he said. "I wanted you. I always wanted you. I was so happy to have a little sister." Shocked, I asked Mike to write his version of my childhood, and this is what he wrote.

Here is my version of Debbie's childhood. Born into a typical nuclear family, Debbie was adored by everyone who knew her from an early age. In every memory I have of Debbie's childhood she was surrounded by friends who enjoyed her company. Mom filled Debbie's childhood with love and attention, taking her to dance, baton, swimming, art, and drama classes on an almost daily basis. I admired Debbie's ability to take on every day with enthusiasm and energy. She was never intimidated by anyone and excelled at everything I can remember. Debbie was mature beyond her years and by age eleven she was modeling and dating older boys. She was a magnet. Everyone wanted to be Debbie's friend and to be wherever Debbie was. There wasn't anything beyond Debbie's reach.

I sat there flabbergasted. I was hearing a perspective I had never even conceived of. Even though I use and embrace my story, I was floored to hear Mike's view. As you can see, asking friends and family members to give us their perspective on our lives' dramas is an effective way to dismantle the limited perspective we believed to be the truth.

Transformation is a shift in perception. It is being able to see something through new eyes. Nothing works quicker to give us a new perspective than seeing the limited view of reality that we thought to be the truth through different sets of eyes. We must understand that our vision—what we can see at any given moment—is limited by our interpretations. The moment we assigned meanings to the events in our lives was the moment we limited our view of reality. Asking other people for their perspectives can reopen the lens through which we view ourselves.

Rewrite your story as though you were an eternal optimist who could see only the light side of your drama. Overemphasize the good points of your story as well as the gifts you were given. How would your life look if seen through the eyes of an angel? The bottom line is that we can take our collective life experiences as a bad memory from which we cannot escape, or we can rewrite them so they provide a valuable foundation from which we can build a fulfilling future. We either learn from the lessons of our past and move forward or dwell on them and stay stuck in the same place.

Learn to recognize clearly when you have stepped back inside your story. To do this, make a list of ten thoughts, feelings, habits, and behaviors you engage in when you are living inside your story. Then make a list of ten thoughts, feelings, habits, and behaviors you engage in when you are living outside your story. What do you have access to when you step outside your story? Finally, make a list of ten ways you can raise your consciousness and step back into your highest self once you recognize that you've slipped back into your story. I asked Helen, a participant in one of my coaching programs, to share her lists.

INSIDE MY STORY...

I overeat.

I drink beer.

I gossip.

I compare myself to others.

I withhold the truth from others and allow resentments to build.

I withhold sex from my husband.

I enroll others in what a victim of life I am.

I criticize and judge myself for everything I do.

I blame my kids for my lack of joy.

I lay around, whining and complaining.

OUTSIDE MY STORY . . .

I decline to gossip.

I relate to people as their highest possibility.

I do yoga.

I express myself freely.

I communicate my feelings and resolve my upsets.

I am grateful for the blessings in my life.

I drink alcohol very rarely, and only one glass at a time.

I am energetic and helpful.

I set a tone of positive energy for my entire household.

I enjoy food, but do not use it as an escape from feeling my emotions.

THINGS I COULD DO TO STEP OUT OF MY STORY

Meditate—for at least fifteen minutes.

Go for a brisk walk.

Garden. Beautify my environment.

Get down on the floor and play with my kids.

Read an inspirational book.

Journal until I reach some deeper understanding.

Call someone whose opinion of me I value.

Give to someone else.

Do yoga.

Feel gratitude for the many blessings in my life.

Use the following quiz to support yourself in staying out of your story. You can tell by the way you feel about yourself and others, by how clearly you see things, and by how you are interpreting your life's events whether you are living inside or outside your personal drama.

Decide whether each of the following statements is true or false.

I feel like my needs aren't being met.

I don't have enough time.

I don't have enough money.

I'm trying, but I just don't get it.

Other people are the cause of my problems.

I find myself thinking, "If only I had more . . ."

I've had the same internal dialogue for more than two weeks.

I believe I don't have a story.

I am engaged in more than one behavior that I know makes me feel bad about myself.

I've called at least one other person this week to enroll them in my pity party.

If you answered "true" to more than four of these statements, you are deeply steeped inside your story. Do not move on without making a commitment to step outside your story. It's important to monitor ourselves and bring conscious awareness to our everyday lives. It's a sad day when we wake up one morning and realize we've been in our story for the past two weeks, two months, or two years. By asking ourselves on a daily basis, "Am I in or out?" we bring the light of our awareness to what has previously been hidden in the shadows.

If you are one of those diehards who find it difficult to let go of your limited self, I recommend that you stand in front of a mirror and repeat your "poor me" story to yourself word for word, until you are so sick of it that you can't bear to repeat it one more time. You'll know that you have succeeded in this exercise if you feel sick to your stomach. However, if you're still not cured, I recommend that you go to a coffee shop and share your story with five strangers. All you have to do is start walking up to people who are sitting alone and say, "I have a great story. Would you like to hear it?" Eventually you'll find someone who is happy to oblige. Then launch into your sad tale, and really get into it. Tell them why and how things have turned out for you the way they have. Show them how nicely a good drama goes with a latte and a baguette. If you still feel attached to the drama of your story, go back to the coffee shop and ask five strangers to tell you their stories. By that time you should be very, very clear that what we're talking about here is a story, that it's only a story and nothing but a story.

If none of the previous exercises has worked, you can always try a good old-fashioned death ceremony. Pretend that you have passed on and someone you love is going to stand up at your funeral and pay tribute to the life you lived inside your story. Write the eulogy that person will give at your funeral. After you read it, ask yourself, "Is this what I am committed to being remembered as?" I asked my girlfriend Colleen to write her eulogy. Here is what she wrote.

Colleen was a very bright girl with a lot of potential. Even though she had a rough start in the beginning of her life, she forged ahead, determined to make something of herself. For some unknown reason she always attracted the wrong jobs, worked for the wrong people, and she certainly never got paid what she was worth. Always there was someone who was preventing her from letting her light shine. If only she had had a break. If only she had had different parents or a better education. If only her talents had been discovered. But instead Colleen kept waiting for that one day when she would be ready to make her mark on the world. But as we sit here today we can see that Colleen never did get that opportunity. Let's all join together in prayer and say, "Poor Colleen!" May she and her story rest in peace.

After you write the eulogy of your story, share it with some friends, have a little ceremony, get some flowers and some food, and lay it to rest.

At every moment you've got to be willing to step outside your story. You must be willing to sacrifice who you know yourself to be for who you can become. You must be willing to give up the smallness of your story for the vastness of your true essence. Every moment you have a choice.

HEALING ACTION STEPS

1. In order to distinguish when you are inside and outside of your story, make a list of the following:

> Ten feelings you have when you are in your story and ten feelings you have when you are out of your story
>
> Ten thoughts you think when you are in your story and ten thoughts you think when you are out of your story
>
> Ten behaviors you engage in when you are inside your story and ten behaviors you engage in when you are out of your story
>
> Ten things you can do to get out of your story when you find that you have slipped back inside

2. Write a letter to your story, honoring it for everything it has taught you and acknowledging that your relationship to it will change as you decide to live outside of its limitations.

3. Create a ritual to say good-bye to your story in the way you have known it. Release it as a way of beating yourself up and keeping yourself small, and welcome it as a resource for fulfilling your purpose in life.

Contemplation

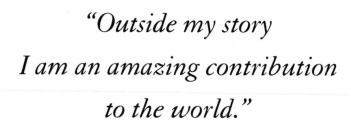

"Outside my story
I am an amazing contribution
to the world."

THE SECRET OF
THE SHADOW

Hidden in the shadow of our stories is a great secret. This secret holds the key to unleashing our magnificence. Our secret is the keeper of abundant joy, unlimited possibility, and Divine bliss. Imagine being the guardian of the earth's rarest and most treasured jewels. As their guardian you would go to any extent possible to protect them. As human beings we do the same thing. Deep inside we know that we are Godly, that we are holy, that we are Divine.

Our greatness, our magnificence, and our light are so valuable that we pile layer on top of layer to protect that which is ours to guard. Because we don't feel safe to expose this part of ourselves, we continually create drama and chaos to hide that which we know should be protected. All of our drama, all of our pain, all of our discontent is hiding the secret of our light. When we have finally grown tired of our stories, when they no longer provide us with any comfort, we are ready to uncover the precious gift that lies within each of us. When we feel we are worthy and can be trusted to take care of our light we will feel free to unleash the greatest power of all: the power of our true nature.

THE HUMAN EXPERIENCE

You and I are explorers, and the terrain we are traveling is our own human experience. If we had chosen to have a Godly experience, a Divine experience, or an otherworldly experience, we would not exist in a human form. But this is not the case. We chose a human experience. And this journey requires us to learn, to grow, to make sense of our very nature. The human experience calls on us to travel the path through the drama of our life stories, through all the false identities we have believed ourselves to be. It requires us to navigate through the realm of emotions in order to deeply understand the mechanism of what it means to be human.

Letting our secrets out allows us to become intimate with our most Divine selves, our spiritual essence. Revealing our secrets merges our humanity with our Divinity. By traveling the path through our stories, by understanding our humanness at the deepest level, we are blessed with the courage to move beyond our personas, to drop our acts, to step out of our stories and stand naked in the presence of our truest selves. Only then will we feel safe enough to stand in all our glory and declare, "This is who I am."

For us to allow our secrets to reign, we must take a warrior's stance in this exploration of our lives. We must dig in, explore, and understand the terrain of our own humanness. For it is only when we truly know and understand ourselves, only when we've traveled the path through our past, that we can throw our arms in the air with the delight and enthusiasm of a child and declare, "I am holy! I am Divine! I am worthy of everything the Universe has to offer." It is only when we've done this vital inner work that we will feel safe enough to let our secrets out for everyone to see.

Often, revealing our secrets leaves us feeling vulnerable and exposed, because we no longer know who we are. It can be terrifying to let go of our false selves, the facades that have been covering up our deeper truth, and expose the essence of our beings. When as children we exposed our lavish gifts, we often were shamed, ignored, or criticized, so as adults we have learned to hide the place in ourselves where we feel the most vulnerable.

But once we expose our secrets, we will see that our dramas and our justifications can no longer protect us. Our intellects can no longer serve us. The only path we can take is one of surrendering to the connection between ourselves and the Divine. Until we feel worthy, until we have sifted through our stories to learn the lessons they have to impart, until we have forgiven ourselves and others, and until we have come to terms with our human struggle, we will always put up some kind of block that keeps us from experiencing our Divinity.

Doing the work in this book has prepared you for the extraordinary journey of living your most Divine life. You are ready now to take the leap outside your story and invite your secret, your sacred light, out of hiding. The process you've gone through to embrace and integrate your story has laid the foundation for you to live a life outside the limitations of your personal drama. If you have done the work outlined in this book, you have identified your story and have come to the profound understanding that you have a story but you are not your story. You have discovered that hidden within your story is a unique recipe, and that by embracing and integrating all aspects of yourself and your life you will find your true purpose. Once you have understood that everything that has happened to you has supported you in gaining the wisdom you need to deliver your unique gift to the world, you can heal your emotional wounds and traumas from the past. You can then begin the process of making peace with your story by looking at the ways you have violated yourself and others and by making the commitment to balance your internal karmic scales.

By cleaning up your past you are able to experience the sacredness of forgiveness, which opens the door to new levels of self-love and deservingness. You no longer feel the need to hide your light out of fear that someone will take it from you. Grounded in the feeling of your own worthiness, you are now free to use all the wisdom you have gathered from your story to bring forth your special gifts to the world. Having found your unique specialty and seen how deeply worthy you are, you are ready to reveal the secret that lies hidden in the shadow of your story. You are ready to acknowledge the deeper truth of who you are. With your gift in hand, you are able to thank your story and appreciate all it has taught you, knowing that it was the very catalyst that opened you to a deeper understanding of what it means to be you. Having done the work, you feel worthy and ready to let down your guard, to let go of your defenses and your persona, and to let your secret stand revealed.

EXPOSING YOUR SECRET

Exposing our secrets makes us feel vulnerable, because they've been hidden for so long. But only when we are willing to be in our vulnerability will we be blessed with the gift of our own light. Sydney sat on the floor of my office, crying. Between sobs she recalled incident after incident from her childhood that left her feeling unlovable, insignificant, disappointed, and left out. There was the time her mother forgot to pick her up from camp and she was the last child there after all the counselors had gone home. There was the time she was left all alone on her birthday. There was the time nobody showed up at her school play and no one told her how cute she looked in her black witch's costume and matching ballet slippers. Being the youngest child in her family, Sydney always had the feeling her opinions didn't matter, and she struggled to be noticed by her parents, who disappointed her more times than she could count. "What did you make their behavior mean about you?" I asked Sydney. More tears came and Sydney answered, "That they don't care about me. That I don't mean anything to them. That I'm nothing. *That I don't matter.*" This was Sydney's story.

Although Sydney is grown up now, with a successful career as a movie producer, inside she is still overwhelmed with the feelings of a five-year-old that remind her that she doesn't matter. Despite all her success and achievements, she is still hungry to be acknowledged. In her career and in her personal life, she strives to be giving and caring, hoping that she will matter enough to the people around her to be worthy of their attention. She is thoughtful and understanding, tries to be a good listener, and is generous with her time and money. Yet, far from the image she projects in the outer world, when Sydney lies in bed at night, she still feels like her life doesn't matter.

When I asked Sydney what the gift of not mattering was, she at first looked at me like I was crazy. "There's no gift in feeling like I don't matter," she said. "What has the feeling of not mattering driven you to do or become?" I asked her. Suddenly Sydney began to see how her whole story and every accomplishment in her life had been driven by the core shadow belief that she doesn't matter. It was that belief that had given Sydney her unique specialty—showing others that they matter—and had driven her to create extraordinary things in the world. Sydney always strives to make movies that she thinks will really matter to her audience. She knows how to bring people together and make them feel important, thus inspiring their best work. Because her life taught her firsthand what it feels like not to matter, she now knows what does matter. Sydney realized that all those painful incidents from her childhood had given her a master's degree in not mattering—which is exactly what has made her unique in her industry. Once Sydney processed the pain that surrounded her shadow belief that she doesn't matter, she could acknowledge her unique specialty and the contribution it makes in the world.

Sydney could see how deeply committed she had been to her story and how she had used it her entire life to deprive herself of the joy of her accomplishments. But now, having uncovered her unique specialty, Sydney felt worthy of her joy and her gifts. I then suggested to Sydney that her story was just a cover-up for the priceless treasure she held. I had Sydney close her eyes, and then I asked her, "What is the secret your story has been hiding?" We sat in silence for several minutes, and then I watched a big smile come across her face as she whispered, "I make a huge difference in the world. I really matter." With clarity and strength Sydney acknowledged that her words were true—that indeed the work she was doing was changing lives. After exposing her secret, Sydney knew she could never go back to living inside the lie of her story again. Standing in the presence of her precious gift, Sydney watched her "I don't matter" story crumble before her eyes. For the first time in her life and her career, she could feel the abundant joy that comes from knowing she makes a profound difference and impact in the world.

Exposing your secret blows your entire story. You might feel that revealing your secret and giving your gifts to the world is an overwhelming responsibility. But this is just another story. Expressing your light is not a responsibility; it's a sacred honor. It takes nothing more than being who you really are, your authentic self. It takes no effort, no making, no struggle. You just have to allow yourself to show up—without your story. If you have never let your light shine bright before, this will most likely feel scary, because as humans we like to hold on to what we know. Standing in the presence of our freedom and our expansiveness can be terrifying, and many of us will unconsciously say, "Give me back my story so I will again know who I am."

STEPPING INTO THE STORM

We have to embrace our vulnerability in order to allow our secret to emerge. We need to take baby steps and learn how to trust. We must learn how to surrender, not to what *we* desire but to what the Universe is showing us. We must trust that if we set out into unknown waters we will be taken to the shore. Imagine what it would be like to stand on a beach and watch a huge gray thundercloud moving toward you, gusty winds howling and huge waves crashing up against the shore. Feeling exhilarated, you imagine how exciting it would be to set sail into the storm, feeling the power of nature and the mystery of the unknown. But a minute later you get scared and your thoughts turn to the safe and predictable choice of finding somewhere to stay covered until the storm blows over. But what if you knew that if you sailed into the storm, armed with all the right gear, on the other side of the rain and winds you would arrive safely on an island filled with great treasures and sparkling jewels? Would you take that journey? Would you trust those who have made their way there before you to give you the support and guidance necessary to find your pot of gold? I ask you to imagine this scenario because exposing the lie of your story and revealing the secret of your shadow can look as dark and scary as sailing into a turbulent storm.

This was true for Laura, a forty-six-year-old woman who has been in a bad marriage filled with pain, abuse, and emotional isolation for more than fifteen years. Everybody who knows Laura is all too familiar with her story: that her marriage is killing her spirit and that her husband doesn't give her the love and attention she deserves. Laura uncovered the shadow belief that held her story together, which echoed the words her father had spoken to her when she was just twelve years old: *You'll never be anything without a man.* Laura had been living that story for the past fifteen years of her life, as though she were a character in a play. When I asked her what secret that story concealed, she said with a smile, "That I am a powerful, independent woman who would be happier living on my own." For a moment Laura stood tall and strong and had a powerful glow coming from her eyes. But within minutes she began to minimize the power of the words she had just spoken and slid back into her familiar story. In the end, Laura was too afraid to let go of the drama she knew so well and opted instead to keep her secret hidden behind the veil of her story.

As is often the case, we sabotage our dreams in the attempt to fit back into the confines of our stories. This is a choice that each of us has to make. We must ask ourselves, "Am I willing to go through some discomfort in order to experience the magnificence of my light, or would I rather stay in the comfort of what I know?" We are the only ones who can tell ourselves it's safe to be in the world without the comfort of our stories. We are the only ones who can make it safe to expose our precious gifts.

DISCOVERING YOUR TRUE ESSENCE

Our stories are the imprint of our existence. They are the unique mark that we leave in this world. When I met Matt he was thirty-two years old, attending his twenty-seventh self-help seminar, and suffering from low self-esteem and feelings of unworthiness. He stood six feet tall, with long blond hair that hung in his face. My first thought about Matt was, *What is he hiding?* I took my hand, pushed his hair out of his face, and asked him what I could do for him. He immediately began telling me his past. He grew up fatherless in a small town and always felt defective because he didn't have a "real" family. Never having much money, he learned early in life how to do without. When Matt was seven years old his mother got into a relationship, which took some of her attention away from him. It was then, Matt told me, that his real problems began. Matt went on for about an hour about how he had gotten into trouble with the law and how by the age of fourteen he was living on the street, hustling to survive. When he was finally faced with a life-threatening case of hepatitis, Matt decided he'd better clean up his act. He began working and saving money, committed to making something of his life.

In his twenties Matt went into the real-estate business, eventually doing well enough that he could buy small houses of his own, fix them up, and sell them for a profit. By the time he was twenty-five he owned over one hundred properties, and by the age of twenty-eight he had finally made it in the big world. With a million dollars in the bank, he began doing bigger projects, and by the time he was thirty-two he had met all his financial goals. But still he suffered. The illusion that having more money or property would bring him happiness was gone, and now he sat before me wondering what to do next. Despite his success, he still found himself engaging in self-sabotaging behaviors, hanging out in places where he didn't want to be, and he couldn't find fulfillment in his personal relationships. Even though he had made it in the material world, inside Matt still felt there was something wrong with him. Matt was lost, wondering where to go and what to do to find the peace he was looking for.

When Matt was finished telling me his tale, I took his hand, looked him in the eye, and told him that the first thing he should do was get a haircut. It was obvious he didn't want anyone to really see him. His hair helped to hide the secret that lay beneath his story that deep down there was something wrong with him. I asked Matt when he was going to stop taking courses and begin teaching them. Matt cocked his head, wrinkled his brow, and looked at me like I was crazy. That was the end of our first meeting.

For the next couple of years I coached Matt on and off. I was taken aback by how bright, sensitive, and intuitive he was. He seemed to have boundless love for all of humanity except himself. Matt constantly tortured himself with his noisy internal dialogue, which screamed, "You're no good, you're defective, and your life doesn't make a difference." Matt would begin most of our sessions by telling me about all the awful things he was up to. He told me that living on the streets at such a young age had made him feel unclean. He had seen too much and done too much, which led him to think about himself as sleazy, damaged, and worthless. Matt's focus was always on what didn't work about himself rather than what did. Little by little I was able to help Matt peel away all the stories that concealed his true essence.

It was obvious to me that Matt was a deeply spiritual man with a great gift to give the world. When I believed he was finally ready to see this about himself, I asked him, "What is the secret that your story conceals?" Matt looked confused. "I wouldn't even begin to know myself without my story," he answered. I sensed that Matt was afraid of looking deeper, so I shared with him the secret my early life story had been concealing. I told him that when I was young and in the clothing business I hung out with a fast crowd whose mantra was "Sex, drugs, and rock 'n' roll." I wanted people to think I was tough and that I knew it all. All I showed in the outer world was my desire for money and status. I spent years trying to hide my sensitivity and my longing for something more. It just didn't seem cool. When I had finally outworn that story I had the sense that I would find peace in a spiritual life. As I grew, I uncovered my deep desire to know God. In the beginning I was embarrassed and ashamed, because being a woman of God certainly didn't fit my image. I didn't want people to know that I was driven to my knees in prayer and that I longed to be an instrument of the Divine. I shared with Matt that the story of my life hid the secret of who I really was. It concealed the truth: that I am a woman of God and I love it.

I could see by the look in Matt's eyes that he understood what I was asking of him. I asked him to take a deep breath and close his eyes, and again I asked the question: "What secret is your story hiding?" With his eyes still closed, Matt blurted out, "The secret that my story is hiding is that I am an innocent and pure expression of spirit." He then opened his eyes and we both sat silent for a long moment, amazed at what had just been revealed. I could see from the clarity in his eyes that he had just connected with his Divine truth. With tears rolling down his checks Matt told me how inside his story he had always seen himself as rotten, sleazy, and damaged—the exact opposite of what he had just heard himself say. In the presence of his purity, Matt was able to see that he could contribute his specialty and give back to the world by teaching what he had learned. Before that moment, Matt had always discounted his wisdom and knowledge, choosing to be a follower and not a leader. But in the presence of his light, Matt was able to see his specialty: teaching teenage boys who are lost and alone how to bring forth their special gifts into the world. Matt had uncovered something very real and very holy. He had revealed the secret hidden in the shadow of his story.

We are the only ones who can make it safe to reveal our secret. No one can protect us from the outside world except ourselves. No one can save us or promise us that we won't be ridiculed or that we won't fail. We probably will fail, and we can be certain that there will be many who will point their fingers at us and project their darkness onto us. But what other choice do we really have? Do we want to stay in the smallness of our stories? Or do we want the authentic gifts that we hold to have an opportunity to shine bright?

For years I was too scared to stand up and claim my piece, to speak out in public, and to share what I know. My ego was so delicate that I feared the disapproval of my peers and the judgments of my detractors. But one day while I was meditating I asked God to give me the courage to surrender my personal fear and allow me to step into a place of Universal service. That evening while I lay in bed I began thinking about the spiritual leaders who had been such a big part of my life and my personal growth. Martin Luther King Jr. came first into my mind. I thought about all the people who loved and honored him as well as all the people who hated and despised him. But what if King had kept his light secret? What if he had hidden his gift from the world? Then I thought of Gandhi. He too had many admirers and many detractors. I wondered what our world would be like without the presence of these men. Suddenly I could see that all those who had a voice or who made a difference in this world had people who loved them and people who hated them. And even though I knew I wasn't a Martin Luther King or a Gandhi, their courage showed me that if I were ever going to make a difference in the world, I too would have to be willing to be both loved and hated. I would have to be able to tolerate criticism as well as praise.

For weeks afterward I found myself thinking about the paradox of it all. I tried frantically to exclude myself from people who had devoted their lives to helping and healing. I tried to tell myself that I was a different type of person, that I was too sensitive and would never be able to handle that kind of ambiguity. I wanted desperately to believe that sharing my gift was not really my purpose.

You, too, have probably told yourself stories about why it is better to keep your secret hidden than to expose it to the ridicule of the world. Maybe you told yourself you couldn't take all the love and admiration that would come your way if you allowed yourself to be truly magnificent. But this is a lie—just another story. None of us is really scared of the praise and the love that are possible if we let our light shine. Even though our brilliance might make us uncomfortable, and even though we might not feel worthy of so much attention, at our core each of us knows that this is our birthright—our authentic expression. Our real fear is the disapproval of others, their harsh judgments, or the withdrawal of their love.

EMBRACING YOUR MAGNIFICENCE

In order to feel safe enough to bare our gifts, we must give up judging ourselves and give up judging others. We must allow ourselves to stand naked without our stories, without our past, without our judgments and justifications. Only then will we know our true essence, and only then will we feel the deep peace of being aligned with our highest selves. Then we can relax, let down our guard, and bask in the glory of our own magnificence.

It is time for us to grow up and be willing to have people not like us. It is time to accept the reality that the approval of others will not give us the security or acceptance we crave. Only the gift within, the Divinely placed purpose, can give us the deep satisfaction of knowing that we are enough, that we are lovable, and that we are profoundly worthy and good. As long as we need the approval of others, we will have to shrink and make ourselves small. When we were little we had a glimmer of how special we are. Then we made it bad. We thought people would hate us if we allowed ourselves to be as big and as special as we are. The real question is, Can we forgive ourselves for our specialness, our gifts, and our uniqueness? And, Can we forgive ourselves for squashing our gifts?

The world needs you. Have you noticed that you're needed? Have you noticed that we could really use your help? I'm talking to you, the part of you that longs to make a difference in the world. This is the time to let your secret be revealed, to mix your recipe, bake your cake, and come out. Join the party. This is your opportunity. You could do it next year, or even in ten years. But I don't think it's an accident that you are reading this book right now. We need you to do your part. We need you to give up your excuses and do your part in this process and in the world.

Now I am asking you to tell me, what is the secret that your story is hiding? Is it that you are Godly? That you are magnificent? That you are worthy beyond measure? That you are pure love? That your life is effortless? What is the secret you've been hiding from yourself and others for all these years?

It's time for you to let your secret out. It's safe now. Maybe it wasn't safe before, but you can take care of it now. Nobody can take it away. Nobody can hurt it. It's time to reward yourself for all the work you've done. Only you can give yourself the permission to honor and hold that secret. Place your hand over your heart and tell yourself that it's safe now to expose your secret. Promise yourself that you will take care of it and hold your secret in the highest regard. Promise yourself that you'll honor and respect it and that you'll deal with anything that comes between you and the precious gift that you hold. Feel what it feels like to now embrace your secret, to take it out of hiding after so many years. This is a time to be very tender with yourself, for you are exposing your most valuable possession. This is a sacred moment, when you reveal your secret for perhaps the first time, when you allow it to be revealed to the world. The time is now.

So now I want you to know that I know your secret. I know

who you are. I know what gifts you bring and what a difference you make in this world. Consider yourself busted, because even though I may not have met you, I know that you hold a precious gift. And I know that it's a very special piece of this Divine puzzle of life—one that no one in the world but you can provide. From the deepest place in my heart I ask you to step out of your story, let your secret be told, and give your precious gift to the world right now.

HEALING ACTION STEPS

1. Set aside some uninterrupted time to do the following visualization. Before getting started, you may want to take a walk or soak in a warm bath to relax yourself. Consider playing some soft music or lighting a candle to create a peaceful mood. Then close your eyes, and begin by allowing your awareness to rest on your breathing. Take a few long, slow, deep breaths, retaining the breath for five seconds or more and then slowly exhaling. Do this four or five times until your mind begins to quiet and settle down.

Call forth an image of yourself as a young child, and imagine that you are feeling happy, safe, and completely carefree. See yourself being fully self-expressed and feeling comfortable in your own being. Spend a few moments breathing into this image, and then ask yourself the following questions, recording your responses in your journal.

When did you hide your secret?

What are you afraid will happen if you let the fullness of your light shine?

How could the people in your family, your workplace, and other areas of your life benefit from you claiming your true magnificence?

2. Write a new story about your life. The theme of this tale is that your light shines bright and the Universe dances in perfect harmony with you. Allow yourself to see how your Divine essence

empowers and inspires all those whose lives you touch. What would your life look like, feel like, and be like if you let your secret out? How would your internal dialogue sound and what messages would you be giving to yourself?

3. Create a power statement that you can repeat to yourself on a daily basis, one that will support you in living your most magnificent life.

4. Identify five daily practices that will support you in letting your light shine.

Contemplation

"I bask in the glory of my most magnificent self."

Acknowledgments

To Liz Perle, my dear friend and editor. Thank you for believing in me and my work. I'm always inspired by the clarity of your vision and the genius of your words.

To Arielle Ford, my sister, who makes my wildest dreams come true. You are my hero. I love and honor you.

To Brian Hilliard and Dharma Dreams, my awesome brother in-law and agent. Thank you for making sure I am taken care of and for being such an inspiring being.

To Danielle Dorman, my very dear friend. Thank you for your great editing skills. You made a huge contribution to this book. I love and appreciate you.

To Katherine Kellmeyer at the Ford Group for being the best publicist anyone could ask for. Thank you for all the years of guidance, support, and dedication.

To my mom, Sheila. Thank you for being the greatest mom and grandma, for loving us all so much and for supporting me in making my dreams come true.

To my brother, Mike Ford, for caring so much about my work. Your wisdom and generosity always inspire me.

To my son, Beau, for always reminding me how precious life is.

To Aunt Pearl—you inspire me every day with your zest for life and your love of our family. I am so grateful for the time we spend together.

To Geeta Singh and the Talent Exchange. I have never felt more supported than I do by you. Thank you for being so impeccable.

To Cheryl Richardson for your extraordinarily generous heart and for all your love, guidance, and friendship.

To Oprah Winfrey for having the courage to bring forth spiritual healing into the world. Thank you for the tremendous opportunities you have given to me and my work.

To Katy Davis for all your support, brilliance, and profound vision.

To Jack Mori for being an extraordinary producer and for having the courage to take on a difficult subject and make it accessible to the world.

To Cindy Goldberg and Stacy Strazis for all the great work you did with me on the *Oprah!* shows. Your big hearts and the love that you brought forth assisted in all the healing that took place. Thank you.

To Sid Ayers for making it possible for me to focus on my writing and on my work. Know that you make a difference.

To Alisha Schwartz. No one has ever cared for me in the way that you do. Thank you for supporting me and for loving Beau so much.

To Steve Hanselman, Margery Buchanan, Eric Brandt, and the entire HarperCollins staff. Working with you is such a joy and pleasure. Each of you brings a unique contribution. You are amazing publishers and I love you.

To Calla Devlin, my publicist at HarperCollins. I love your light and your enthusiasm. You are a dream to work with.

To Lisa Zuniga for your commitment to making this book great. It has been an honor to work with you.

To Carl Walesa for your awesome copyediting. Thank you.

To Stephen Samuels for stepping up and being big enough to lead this work into the world. You are doing a tremendous job and making a huge difference in thousands of lives.

To the beloved participants of my coaching programs. I have never met a more committed and extraordinary group of individuals. Each of you makes a huge difference in my life and in my work.

To Cliff Edwards for making such a huge difference in so many people's lives. Thank you for your profound commitment to healing yourself and this world.

To Justin Hilton. How privileged I am to have you as my dear friend and spiritual partner. You're an extraordinary man.

To Patrick Dorman. Thank you for stepping outside your story and exposing the magnificence of your being. I am truly honored to be on this journey with you.

To Luba Bozanich. Your extraordinary commitment to transcend pain and suffering is a great inspiration to me. Thank you for being who you are.

To Bea Bigman. Your light and your love always bring a smile to my face. Thanks for all that you have given to the community of people that I love so much.

To Neale Donald Walsch, Deepak Chopra, and Marianne Williamson for being such amazing, supportive friends and teachers.

To Divina Infusino for supporting me in getting organized and helping to bring this book to fruition. Your passion for this work inspired me.

To Rabbi Moshe Levin, who so generously shares his vast wisdom with me. Thank you for the love and support you offer to me and my family.

To David Simon and the entire staff of The Chopra Center for Well Being. Thank you for all your love, support, and devotion in bringing this work out into the world.

To Jeremiah Sullivan for always rising up to the occasion and catching me at my best. To Robert Bennett for being such a wonderful perfectionist. I love my picture.

To Natalie Snyder and Tony Fiorentino for allowing me to wallow in my "hair story" and for loving me anyway. You are both brilliant artists.

To Henrietta Rosenberg. Thank you for being such an amazing yoga guru and for always being there for me.

To the Coffee Cup Restaurant and its magical owner, Marla Reif, for providing great food and a cozy corner to edit the pages of this book.

To the wise and generous souls who so openly shared their lives so that others could be transformed by their stories. Thank you for your huge contribution to this book.

To the Spirit that talks to me, guides me, loves me, and enables me to do what I do in the world. Thank you for your assistance. I am honored to be of service.

To contact Debbie Ford and for information on her workshops:

Debbie Ford
P.O. Box 8064
La Jolla, CA 92038
800-655-4016
www.debbieford.com

In loving memory of Paige Farley Hackel,
who had the courage to live outside her story.
You will live forever in the hearts of your community
at the Ford Institute for Integrative Coaching.